Abolition a Sedition by a Northern Man

by

Calvin Colton

Abolition a Sedition by a Northern Man
by Calvin Colton

ISBN: 978-93-59955-86-5

Published by

DOUBLE 9 BOOKS

2/13-B, Ansari Road
Daryaganj, New Delhi – 110002
info@double9books.com
www.double9books.com
Tel. 011-40042856

ABOUT THE AUTHOR

Calvin Colton, born on September 14, 1789, in Longmeadow, Massachusetts, and passing away in 1857 in Savannah, Georgia, become an exquisite American creator, clergyman, and educator at some stage in the nineteenth century. He played a multifaceted role in his lifetime, leaving a substantial mark at the non-secular and literary panorama of his generation. Colton commenced his profession as a priest and served as a pastor in various church buildings, contributing to the religious discourse of the time. He became known for his sturdy evangelical beliefs and frequently wrote on religious subjects, emphasizing moral values and Christian concepts. In addition to his religious interests, Colton turned into a prolific writer and lecturer. He authored several books and essays, inclusive of "Lacon: Or, Many Things in Few Words," which have become one in all his most well-known works. "Lacon" is a collection of moral and philosophical aphorisms, reflecting Colton's deep contemplation on existence, ethics, and human nature. His writings were characterized through their concise and idea-upsetting nature. Calvin Colton's impact prolonged past his literary contributions. He additionally played a function in training, serving as a professor and administrator at various establishments. His work in the fields of faith, literature, and education made him a prominent figure of his time and left a lasting legacy inside the highbrow and religious realms of nineteenth-century America.

CONTENTS

PREFACE..7

CHAPTER I
THE CHARACTER OF THE ABOLITION ORGANIZATION............ 9

CHAPTER II
THE AMERICAN ANTI-SLAVERY SOCIETY
A SEDITIOUS ORGANIZATION 20

CHAPTER III
THE SEDITIOUS CHARACTER OF THE ANNUAL REPORT OF
THE AMERICAN ANTI-SLAVERY SOCIETY OF 1838 29

CHAPTER IV
THE SEDITIOUS CHARACTER OF THE AMERICAN
ANTI-SLAVERY SOCIETY FARTHER CONSIDERED 35

CHAPTER V
VIOLENT REFORMS, AND THEIR CONNEXION
WITH ABOLITIONISM 43

CHAPTER VI
THE ABOLITION ORGANIZATION BORROWED
FROM THE RELIGIOUS WORLD.. 48

CHAPTER VII
THE ANARCHICAL PRINCIPLES OF ABOLITIONISM 51

CHAPTER VIII
THE INCENDIARY DOCTRINES OF ABOLITIONISM 56

CHAPTER IX
POLITICAL RESPONSIBILITY IN REGARD TO SLAVERY.............. 61

CHAPTER X
THE ROMANCE OF ABOLITIONISM.. 69

CHAPTER XI

EVERY MAN MIND HIS OWN BUSINESS 76

CHAPTER XII

PERFECTIONISM 79

CHAPTER XIII

LIBERTY AND EQUALITY 83

CHAPTER XIV

SOCIAL AND POLITICAL EFFECTS OF ABOLITIONISM 88

CHAPTER XV

THE BAD EFFECTS OF ABOLITIONISM ON
THE FREE COLORED POPULATION, AND ON
THE CONDITION AND PROSPECTS OF SLAVES 91

CHAPTER XVI

A HYPOTHETICAL VIEW OF ABOLITIONISM 95

CHAPTER XVII

ABOLITIONISM CONSIDERED AS PROPOSING NO
COMPENSATION FOR SLAVE-PROPERTY 97

CHAPTER XVIII

THE CONDITION OF AMERICAN SLAVES AS COMPARED
WITH OTHER PORTIONS OF THE AFRICAN RACE 105

CHAPTER XIX

THE EXAMPLE OF QUAKERS, OR SOCIETY OF FRIENDS 114

CHAPTER XX

THE SOUTH HAVE DONE WITH ARGUMENT 116

CHAPTER XXI

REASONS WHY THE ABOLITION MOVEMENT,
UNDER ITS PRESENT ORGANIZATION, MUST
SUCCEED IN OVERTHROWING THE GOVERNMENT 118

CHAPTER XXII

THE ABOLITION ORGANIZATION DESTRUCTIVE
OF REPUBLICAN LIBERTY 123

PREFACE

We trust it will be obvious to all, that it was impossible to treat Abolitionism according to its merits, or to exhibit its true character, without regarding it as a religious movement. There are two prominent features of the moral and religious history of our country, with which we have been compelled to come in contact. We, therefore, take this opportunity so far to explain, as to bar the accident of being misapprehended. First, then, we have averred the philosophical connexion of antecedent and consequence between *Abolitionism* and *violent reforms*. It is proper, therefore, that we should state how much we are willing to be understood as meaning by this couplet of terms, having such a relation to the subject of this work. We say, then, that by *violent reforms*, we mean those religious and moral agitations of our country, which have proved alike unfriendly to religious and social order, which are generally disapproved by sober Christians, and we believe by the great majority of Christians, of all, or nearly all, denominations. It is possible, that on a single point we have hit hard a cherished opinion of many persons, for whom we have the greatest respect; but as it relates merely to a *mode* of action, we must claim to be indulged in our own opinion in that matter, as we allow the same privilege to others.

In the next place, we have found it necessary, in the *exhibit* we have made of the political machinery of the Abolition movement, to enquire into its origin; and it will be manifest to all, that it was brought from the religious world. The fact, that the model of the American Anti-slavery Society was borrowed from the Religious and Benevolent Society system, could not implicate those institutions, in the estimation of the public, unless they should see fit to follow the same example, and so far as they might do it, by going over from the religious and moral, into the political sphere; which, we trust, they will be wise enough not to do. It was necessary to describe the machinery of those Societies in order to give the true picture of the one under particular consideration; but we have taken care at the same time to state, that the American Anti-slavery Society has betrayed and violated the principles of the Religious and Benevolent Society system, by first assuming its model, and then passing over into the field of political action. That all these machineries are well adapted to political ends, whenever they may be perverted and applied in that direction, it is unnecessary to say; and the only way to escape the charge, is to avoid the fault. The Abolition Society has gone openly into that field, on which account we have considered it fair and exactly true to represent it as a *political organization*, and as being necessarily such from the work it has taken in hand.

Having, therefore, explained on these two points, we submit the work, without farther comment, to speak for itself.

January 1, 1839.

CHAPTER I
THE CHARACTER OF THE
ABOLITION ORGANIZATION

There seems to have been a uniform impression among the great majority of the citizens of the United States, that the Abolition movement in this country is wrong, as it stands related to our political fabric; but the exact character and extent of this wrong have not been so well defined in the public mind, as to enable the people to see how a remedy can be applied to arrest and control the mischief that appears to be growing out of this agitation. Every reflecting person in the land sees and feels, that it threatens to break asunder the American Union; and few doubt, that such will be the result, if it is permitted to go on. We take for granted, that the almost unanimous voice of the whole country would concur in the opinion, that a violent dissolution of the American Republic would be the greatest calamity that could happen in this Western world. Can it be, then, that there is no Constitutional power to suppress an organization, the rise and course of which tend so directly and so inevitably to the disruption and demolition of the Federal Government? Certainly, it would be a great and notable defect in the political structure of the United States, if there were to be found in it no principle of conservation against such a danger, and if the people of this country were compelled to see an enemy start up among themselves, and march directly to the overthrow of the Government, without any power to resist. Doubtless, in a last resort, the Union is too dear to the American people generally to allow it to be sacrificed without an attempt to maintain it, even if there should prove to be no provision in the Constitution and laws. The necessity and importance of the case would create a law for the occasion. The people would feel, that they have a better right to defend the Union, than an enemy has to destroy it. But if the law of necessity be waited for, the scale of chances as to the final issue may have become doubtful—too doubtful and too portentous to be prudently staked on such a hazard; and the American Union might be lost forever.

If, however, it can be shown, that the Abolition movement is at war with the genius and letter of the National Constitution and of the Constitutions of the States respectively, and with that social compact which created the

Union, and under which it has hitherto been maintained, then clearly there will be presented a Constitutional basis on which this movement can be opposed, and by which, if it shall become necessary, it can be suppressed. We propose an attempt to establish the position, that such *is* the character of this movement, and consequently, that there is a remedial power against its action in the Constitution and laws of the land.

Before we proceed to an array of the law which applies to the case, it may be useful to inquire into the nature and character of the organization, under which the Abolition movement is carried on. As this machinery is so well known to the public, it will only be necessary to refer to such general facts as the Abolitionists themselves will not deny, however they may differ from us in the character and name ascribed to them as a whole.

We observe, then, that the American Anti-Slavery Society, under the authority and by the action of which, this movement is conducted, is a *grand and permanent political organization, self-elected, self-governed, independent, and irresponsible, having no connexion with the Government of the country, but yet usurping the appropriate business of that Government.*

It is an *organization*. This, certainly, will require no proof, as nobody will deny it. It is formed after the model of the Religious and Benevolent Society system, which has been in action for about thirty years past, and which, in the later parts of this period, has grown into considerable importance in the United States and in Great Britain. The social influence of this system has been much greater in this country than in the father land. But so long and so far as it was confined to religious and benevolent objects, the political authorities and feeling of the community seem to have taken little or no alarm. It was obvious, from experience and observation, that these organizations were armed with a wide spread, and many of them with an all pervading influence; and that they were admirably calculated to acquire power, and to bring to bear an efficient and energetic action on their specific objects. In their history and progress, as their exigencies have seemed to require, they have severally erected a sort of State machinery, with a Constitution as a general basis of polity; with the customary law-making, executive and judicial powers; with principal and under secretaries; with a fiscal department; and with numerous subsidiary agencies, according to the nature and extent of their operations. Some of these institutions are engaged in enterprises as wide as the globe, have numerous foreign establishments of no mean consideration, and foreign colonies have been erected and are governed by them. Nothing but a state machinery, with a corresponding polity, was adequate to the execution of such designs. And while they were confined to religious and benevolent operations, they had not excited the jealousy of the political world; at least, so far as we know, not to any considerable extent.

And it may be remarked—as we shall have occasion hereafter to notice more particularly—that the Abolition movement, under its present organization, originated in religious sentiment, and commenced as a benevolent enterprise. It was natural, therefore, in view of the success which had attended these other institutions, and of the great power and efficiency they had acquired over the public mind, to adopt the same model—the same sort of State machinery in the several departments of its organization. And thus, in the American Anti-Slavery Society, we have an independent and powerful Commonwealth, organized, like every other State, on the basis of a Constitution declarative of its great and fundamental principles, with a head, with a cabinet, with its various State departments and secretaries, with a productive and regular system of fiscal operations, with a polity of its own, with a vast republic of subsidiary combinations, multiplying rapidly, and each constantly increasing in numbers and influence, acquiring talent, wealth, and power on a large scale, creating and sending forth upon the public a world of literature of its own chosen character, in the various forms of books, periodicals, journals, tracts, and pictorial representations; and able, on the principle of such an organization, while unresisted by any opposing power, to extend and wield an influence, which, sooner or later, will dissolve the Union, and send the Government of this proud Republic, in broken fragments, to the winds of heaven.

And it is a *political* organization. It is true, indeed, that when Abolition first broke out in New York, in 1834, the most prominent leaders there disclaimed all participation in political matters, as will appear from the following note, unless it is to be regarded as a *ruse de guerre* for the occasion: "It has been our object to address the hearts and consciences of our fellow citizens, and to defend our principles by facts and arguments; to encourage the people of color to great circumspection of conduct and forbearance; *and to abstain from mingling the objects of our society with either of the political parties.*"

Signed, "Arthur Tappan, John Rankin, E. Wright, jr., Joshua Leavitt, W. Goodell, Lewis Tappan, Samuel E. Cornish.

New York, July 16th, 1834."

The following *Circular*, from the Anti-slavery office in New York, issued for electioneering purposes, in the New York political campaign of 1838, would seem to show, that great advances have been made in regard to the political character of this society, since 1834:—

"Dear Sir,

"Enclosed you have a list of the publications of this society, to which you will please direct any of our *Whig* friends, who may desire a knowledge of the *truth*. I am gratified that our Abolition friends are to be found on the *Whig side*, rather than the *Loco Focos*; for the cause of the country and of humanity ought to go together. *If we can rivet ourselves firmly on one of these parties, we can gain our object. Be careful.*

I am yours, &c. per Arthur Tappan.

B. Le Roy."

New York, Nov. 1, 1838.

This *Circular* was addressed to P. W. Wesley, jr., and marked No. 126. How many *more* were sent out, of course we do not know—it might be *hundreds*, or it might be *thousands*.

It is no more than fair, however, to observe, that Mr. Arthur Tappan has disclaimed having authorized Mr. Le Roy the use of his name in this instance; which, indeed, is of very little consequence, and in no way affects the object we have in view by these references. Whether the gentlemen, who signed the note of July 16, 1834, were really so blind as not to see the *necessary* connexion of their cause with politics, we cannot pretend to say. If they *did* see it, their disclaimer, to say the least, was unbecoming. As men of common discernment, they *ought* to have known as well then as now, that they could do nothing in this business, in the way they propose, without affecting the politics of the country; and that the movement *in toto*, from beginning to end, is political in its character and bearings. Certainly, since that time, the Abolitionists have better learned the position which they occupy. What shall we say? That their early disclaimer was a cloak to conceal their designs? We would rather suppose, that they did not know what they were about. Would, that we could say, they are equally ignorant now, that thereby they might be proved more innocent. Evidently, the disguise, if disguise it was, is thrown aside. By their own public avowals and acts, official and other, they are now fairly and openly in the political field. The following resolution was passed at the Annual meeting of the American Anti-Slavery Society, at New York, May, 1838: "*Resolved*, that we deprecate the organization of any Abolition political party; but that we recommend to Abolitionists throughout the country, to interrogate candidates for office, with reference to their opinions on subjects connected with the abolition of slavery; and to vote, irrespective of party, for those only who will advocate the principles of universal liberty."

Three of the Corresponding Secretaries of this Society, James G. Birney, E. Wright, jr., and Henry B. Stanton, issued a circular from the office at New York, in July 1838, to Agents in the country, quoting the above resolution, and remarking, that "resolutions embodying the same idea have been passed by the New England Anti-Slavery Convention, and we believe, by nearly all, if not all, the State Anti-Slavery Societies;" and that "they think the time has come, when the friends of the slave, throughout the free States, should act fully up to the letter and the spirit of these resolutions. We hope, therefore, you will, without delay, confer with Abolitionists in your region on the subject, by correspondence, by holding meetings, and in such other ways as may be deemed expedient, and take prompt and efficient measures, *to secure the election of such candidates for the National and State Legislatures*, as the friends of the slave can cheerfully support. By order of the Executive Committee."

The following is an extract from a letter written by Mr. Stanton, one of the Secretaries who signed the above Circular, showing how well he himself had been engaged in these duties: "From Lockport I returned to Utica. By request I delivered an address in the Bleeker street Church, the evening of the 10th inst. *on the political duties of the 40,000 Abolition voters in this State,* (New York) *with reference to the fall elections.*"

The following are extracts from the public, well considered, authoritative and solemn document of the Annual Report of the American Anti-Slavery Society for 1838:—"It is often said, that religion has nothing to do with our republican politics; and hence it is inferred, that a cause which is based upon and inseparable from religion, should not presume to meddle with political affairs. But to make the proposition true, we must read instead of *religion, sectarianism....* The religious principles of Abolitionism have nothing to do with *sects....* They are but the thoughts and opinions of all who truly love God.... Abolitionism *must* have much to do with politics.... Abolitionists have resolved, *from the first*, to act upon slavery *politically....* During the year this principle has produced the happiest results. The candidates of the opposing parties have been questioned, and their answers published; and in cases too numerous to mention, the election has resulted in favour of those who most decidedly pledged themselves to Anti-Slavery measures."

The *religious* character of Abolitionism, as here confessed, will be considered in a subsequent place. We do not dissent from the suggestion conveyed, that religion has its political *rights*, under the Constitution, as much as any other interest, feeling, or principle; but we do not see the force of the distinction drawn between *religion* and *sectarianism* for this particular purpose; although the distinction is in fact obvious. Are not Abolitionists a *sect*, and as strongly marked as any that can be named? They fall, therefore, under the ban of their own rule. But, although religion has its political *rights*, not excepting even *sectarianism*—and we have yet to learn that there is any religion in the country, which is not sectarian, both in its principles and modes of operation, not only in relation to other religious bodies, but to Christianity itself, the catholic standard—it must yet be very careful not to usurp political *powers* in this country—not to have *too much* "to do with our republican politics." "Abolitionism *must* have much to do with politics." The word "must," is italicised in the Report, and *may*, therefore, be taken as intended to be emphatically significant. We agree with them perfectly. But, that "Abolitionists have resolved, *from the first*, to act upon slavery *politically*," is a matter which they must settle among themselves, inasmuch as when they *first set out*, they disclaimed it, as would appear from the note of July 16th, 1834, above introduced.

Our object in these quotations, is not to inform the public generally in regard to facts of this kind, as they are sufficiently well known—but merely to throw out a few tangible materials, connected with volumes of the same class, which might easily be collected, for the purpose of justifying in our pages the conclusions we deduce from them. We will trouble our readers with but one more which is from a *clerical* Agent of the Society in the western part of New York, dated Aurora, Oct. 8, 1838. It is a letter to a fellow laborer in Chetauque County.

> "Dear Sir,
>
> "I have just had assigned to me, by the Executive Committee of the New York State Anti-Slavery Society, as my field of labor for several months to come, Niagara, Erie, Chetauque, and Cataraugus Counties. The first object to which I am bending all my energies, is the holding of County meetings *before the coming election, with a view especially of preparing and exciting Abolitionists to carry their principles to the polls, and wield all their* political, *as well as moral and religious power* for the redemption, &c. ... Can you not create a *tremendous reaction* at this time, &c.? ... The only way in which we can move the proslavery and dough-faced politicians, is by showing them our *political strength*, &c.... Now, will you call together your Executive Committee, and fix on a time and place for a Convention? Let me know immediately, and write letters all over the County,—*have notices given out in the* Churches, &c. ... and have town Abolition Meetings held before the County Convention.
>
> "Yours for the crushed slave,
>
> "T. M. Blakesley."

These extracts may serve to indicate the zeal and activity of the Secretaries and numerous Agents of this society, *clerical* and other, previous to the New York elections, and the modes adopted to secure their ends. The interrogation of "candidates for the National and State Legislatures," and for other civil and political stations, as resolved upon and recommended by the parent Society, has been scrupulously carried out. The correspondence between Messrs. Seward and Bradish on the one side, and the official organs of the Society on the other, while these two gentlemen stood before the people of the State of New York as candidates, the first for Governor, and the second for Lieutenant Governor, has been laid before the public—all tending to the same point. Not being exactly satisfied with the result of the election in New York, so far as it demonstrated the influence of the Anti-Slavery Society, it has been suggested by Gerritt Smith, Esq., who seems to be a sort of Dictator General in these matters, that the Abolition societies should undergo a new organization, with a view to the expurgation of the baser and unsound materials, by requiring the despotic test of binding the conscience in the use of the elective franchise. How this will go down, we are unable to say; though it seems to us to be carrying matters with a high hand. Doubtless, the business, in one form or another, will go ahead, in despite of the imprudence of individuals, until the people of this country can be made to see the real character and tendency of the movement. Suffice it to say, as is sufficiently evident, that the American Anti-Slavery Society is now a *grand political organization*, aiming, by the use of political agencies and powers, at a radical and great change in the American political fabric. We shall yet have occasion to show, that this change, urged in this mode and under present circumstances, unless the movement can be checked and suppressed, must necessarily and inevitably dissolve the Union, and consequently overthrow the Government, as it now exists. But our immediate object is to establish the proposition, as stated in *Italics* on page 3, in order to prepare the way for the application of those principles of American Constitutional law, which will prove this Society to be a *seditious organization*.

The most essential point of the proposition now under consideration, is the fact, that the American Anti-Slavery Society is a *political* organization. That, we think, may be regarded as already established; but it may still be fortified by the consideration, that it is *necessarily* so from the object it has in view, apart from the position it has assumed before the public by its own avowals and measures, and by the agencies it has taken in hand. Slavery, as is well known, and as will hereafter be made apparent by the introduction of authorities, is a corporate part of the American political fabric, established by Constitutional law, and interwoven with the frame of the Federal Government. It is not only a thoroughly pervading element, and main pillar of political society in the slave-holding States, but it is made a part of the supreme law of the land in the Federal Constitution. It is impossible, therefore, from the nature of the case, to institute any action, private or public, individual or combined, in any form, or by any agency, to abolish or eradicate slavery from American society, which will not be of a political character. Consequently, the Abolition movement, which, as before remarked, originated in religious sentiment, which was prompted and is still sustained principally by religious men, and which borrowed the model of its organization from the action of the religious world, by instituting an exact copy, the moment it entered the field, was transformed into a political body from the very nature of the work it had undertaken, notwithstanding it was, and still is, actuated by religious sentiment. It is nevertheless political, and it is all the more dangerous, because religion is in it—not Christianity. We shall by and by attempt to show the difference between Christianity and that religion, which lies at the bottom, and is the instigator, of this movement. We have seen, that, in the first setting out, the leaders professed to disclaim political alliance; but, allowing they were sincere in that disclaimer, they soon discovered it was a false step. Throwing aside all disguise, they have now gone *the whole* for political action. At first, they were timid, perhaps—did not know their strength, which might be a reason for not coming out under their own flag. But, *crescit eundo*—the cause soon obtained sympathy, and found way to importance; and behold! it dares to face the Government of the country in open conflict, and to erect its batteries against that Constitutional fabric, which has hitherto been so dear to American citizens.

We have stated, that this political organization is *permanent*. The meaning under which we propose to sustain the application of this epithet in this case, refers, by contradistinction, to a mode of popular political action, which, we conceive, is authorised by the Constitutional law of the land, and which proves equally, that a *permanent* organization of this kind is unauthorised and prohibited. For the present we simply state, what we suppose will not be contradicted, that the American Anti-Slavery Society is a *permanent* body, in distinction from those popular assemblages or conventions, which are customarily held in this country for political purposes, under the specific sanction of the Constitution and laws, which exist only for the time being, which do not presume to arm themselves with a distinct and separate polity, or to set up an imperium in imperio, independent and irresponsible.

We have stated also, that it is a *grand* political organization. This term is of no farther importance than simply to indicate, what is very well known, that this Society is great and powerful. It claims to wield 40,000 of the political votes of the State of New York. Whether this be over or under the true estimate, we take it from themselves; and it is probably fair to conclude, that they are equally strong in most of the other free States. Admitting that they have one-half, or even one-fourth, of this power, it is enough to justify the application of this term. It is a *grand* organization also, in consideration of its vast and complicated machinery, of the variety and extent of its operations, and of its means of influence. In 1838, this Society reports 1350 auxiliaries, of which 12 were State Societies, now 13, and 340 of these organized in the course of the previous year; 38 travelling Agents, so constantly engaged, as to have performed jointly 27 years' labour in one; 75 local lecturers, circulating in adjacent towns, as far as convenient; money raised in the course of the year, $40,000, being $5,000 in excess of the previous year, notwithstanding the pecuniary embarrassments of the community; the issues of the press, 187,316 copies of Human Rights, 193,800 of the Emancipator, 42,100 Circulars and Prints, 12,054 bound volumes, 72,732 Tracts and Pamphlets, 97,600 of the Slaves' Friend, and 40,000 of the Anti-Slavery Record. Total: 646,502.

This society, therefore, is a *grand*, and in its moral and political influence, a stupendous machinery.

And it is *self-erected, self-governed, independent*, and *irresponsible*. The truth of these statements, we think, is self-evident in all that we intend, or desire to be understood, by them. The first, certainly, is true. For what authority, independent of its component parts, suggested, or sanctioned it? And the second is equally true. For, where is the power, out of itself, that dictates, or controls, its proceedings? The third and fourth are also true. For what authority will they acknowledge, as competent to call them to account? They are, indeed, responsible to public opinion; but the relation we intend to express, is responsibility to some constituted authority; and in this view our proposition is sustained, so far as their designs are concerned. We presume they do not recognize the right of any known authority to call them to account. We think it fair, therefore, to represent this Society as *self-erected, self-governed, independent*, and *irresponsible*. So far as our individual opinion is concerned, we do indeed believe and hold, that they are responsible to an authority that is competent to act upon them, when a sense of public duty may require it, and that it is sufferance only that screens the action of this Society from uncomfortable rebuke. But we mean only to assert in our proposition, what we suppose is true: that they do not *hold* themselves responsible; that there is no constituted, or official, connexion between them and a superior power; and that they consider themselves entitled to carry on the operations in which they are engaged, under their present organization, without check, control, or interference of any authority.

Moreover, *there is no such connexion between them and the Government of the country,* as is prescribed by constitutional law to popular assemblages, or associations, for political purposes. There is, indeed, no connexion at all. The government is not even advised of the existence of this society by its own official acts; at least we have never heard of it.

And yet further—which is the last point of our proposition—this society *has usurped the appropriate business of the Government.* They have formally and solemnly declared, in various forms, so far as their authority goes, that slavery is wrong by a higher and more imperative law than that of the country, and set themselves directly to do it away, by all the means they can employ, in the application of a stupendous machinery of their own creation, and under their own independent control. The elective franchise is only one means, and as yet by far the least efficient. Without any balance of influence to oppose and counteract the effect of their proceedings on the public mind, they have been enabled, by the advantages and power of their organization, to agitate the whole country, to throw the South into a state of consternation, and to menace the overthrow of the Government. No one doubts—and therefore we think we are justified in saying—that, had it not been for the necessary posture of self-defence, assumed by the slave-holding States, the Agents of this Society, without waiting for the action of Government, would have carried their incendiary measures directly into the South, and raised a servile insurrection and civil war. It is true, indeed, that this Society have commenced working hard at the polls, as a means of accomplishing their end, and so far have recognized the principle, that Government is to be consulted. But all their other operations, which comprehend the principal sum of their labors, have been of a character which would seem to imply, that the removal of slavery was their business. They have never entered on that course of action for a change in the political fabric of the country, which Constitutional law prescribes, by acting on the Government, the only legitimate organ. They have not even approached the Government, nor recognised either its existence or authority for such a purpose. We speak of the action of the Society *as such,* and not of the action of its individual members in their capacity as citizens. If citizens, desiring such an object, are required to address the Government, instead of seeking to undermine the Constitution and laws, by indirect and independent operations; and if this rule has been wisely enacted for the public peace and safety, much more is it incumbent on a powerful combination, in undertaking to change the laws of the country—if it be lawful for such a combination to be formed—to advise the Government of their wishes and proceedings. Just in proportion as they are more influential and more powerful than individuals, by virtue of association, is it more incumbent on them, and more important, to consult the regular and constituted authorities.

But what has been the fact in regard to the operations of the American Anti-slavery Society? Simply, that they have gone to this work just as if it were their own proper business—as if there were no government in the land. They have never addressed the Government; they have never consulted it; they have never asked leave to be, to act, or to enter this field; but have erected a republic of their own, with a State machinery, and set themselves to change the government of the country, as if it devolved upon them by original and indefeasible right. In a word, they have taken in hand, by a virtual usurpation, the most delicate, and the most disturbing political question, which could possibly be agitated—a question, which, by the Constitutional frame of our Government, belongs properly and only to the States where slavery exists, and which, for that reason, the General Government itself can never meddle with, without the consent of those States. Clearly, the National Government is the only channel through which the subject can be lawfully approached from the free States; by the Federal compact the National Government is the public guardian of slavery; and consequently, when ever its abolition is attempted under the jurisdiction of the United States, independent of the action of the General Government, and without the consent of the slave States, it is a direct invasion of chartered rights, and a usurpation.

We have now done with the proposition laid down for the argument of this chapter, and will only repeat it in form for the consideration of the reader: *That the American Anti-slavery Society is a grand and permanent political organization, self-erected, self-governed, independent, and irresponsible, having no connexion with the Government of the country, but yet usurping the appropriate business of that government.*

CHAPTER II
THE AMERICAN ANTI-SLAVERY SOCIETY
A SEDITIOUS ORGANIZATION

We have shown, in the previous chapter, that the American Anti-slavery society is a *permanent political organization*, attempting to effect a change in the government of the country, by its own independent, and we may add, sovereign, operations. We now propose to show, that such an organization, under such independent and irresponsible action, is unconstitutional and illegal, and consequently seditious. Even if there were no law in the case, we suppose the sovereignty of a nation, in other words, of the majority of the people, in a government constituted like ours, is competent to interpose their authority to prevent the damage of the Republic in an unforeseen exigency. So far as Constitutional law is provided, it is the rule; but where it is wanting, necessity becomes law, to be used in the best discretion of the constituted authorities, in all emergencies in which the safety of the public may demand such a resort. This is the original and undisputed right of that sovereignty, which is always supposed to be vested in a national and independent government. It is of the nature of original legislation for a supposed occasion. It is the use of a right, and a violation of no law, inasmuch as no law exists that is applicable to the case.

But, fortunately, and to bar all controversy, there *is* a law provided for the case now under consideration. It is well known—it is written in the characters of blood on the pages of our history—that our fathers fought and died to secure the right of the people to a representation in the Government, and to be heard by the government, whenever they feel the pressure of an evil demanding the interposition and action of the public authorities, before a remedy can be applied, in the usual forms of legislation, as the result of the use of the elective franchise. But it is not to be forgotten, that the most desirable, the most quiet, and the most salutary action of Government, is the regular and uniform routine of its legislative, executive, and judicial functions, as constituted for general purposes. But the experience of history proves, that public exigencies may arise, when the action of Government may be required out of the usual course; or when the measures of a Government may operate so uncomfortably and oppressively on the people, as to furnish occasion for an expression of their will, before it can be conveyed through the channel of the elective franchise. The Constitutional law of our country, both of the Federal Government and of the States, has provided for these occasions; and in that particular afforded an eminent advantage over that despotic sway of absolute monarchies, which rebukes and suppresses the expressions and interferences of the popular will. The most valuable right of our free institutions is the choice of our own rulers. Next to that, is the right of instructing them in a knowledge of what the people desire. For the conveyance of this will two Constitutional channels have been opened; one in the elective franchise, and the other by the right of petition and remonstrance. The use of both these rights is always supposed to have a direct and immediate connexion with the Government: the first appoints the Government, and the second instructs it. And there rights are found to be sufficient, because, if a Government refuses to respect the popular will, fairly expressed and well ascertained, the people have their remedy in the franchise. They can appoint such rulers as will do their pleasure. Hence there is never a necessity, and there can be no apology, for the dangerous resort to permanent political combinations, acting under an organized polity, independent of the Government of the country, having designs upon that Government, either to control its counsels, or to affect a change in its structure. But such precisely, as will be seen, is the American Anti-slavery Society.

Moreover, it is inconsistent with the *genius* of a Constitutional government, that such an organization should be permitted to arise in its bosom, and make war upon it by original, usurped, and independent functions. The Constitution of a nation knows no rival, admits of none, within its own jurisdiction. It would be the same as to sanction sedition and treason; it would be forging the weapons of its own destruction, and turning a suicidal hand upon itself. The empire claimed, and designed to be maintained, by a Constitutional government, like that of the United States, is *sole*. It cannot, without peril to itself, admit a rival political and independent power on the same territory. But such is the American Anti-slavery Society. It is an independent Commonwealth, a republic *within* the Republic, a State, having all the machinery of a State which its exigencies require, and is perpetually adding to that machinery, without limit, and without control. It has already proved sufficiently powerful to disturb the peace of the country, to endanger the lives of its citizens, and to threaten a dissolution of the Union; and who can say, that it will not revolutionise the government, and introduce anarchy and desolation? Such is the prospect, and such are the most sober convictions of discerning and far seeing minds, if it is permitted to go on.

But let us look to the law which applies to the case. The Constitution of the United States, and in accordance with that, the Constitutions of the several States, in the same manner, and in like terms, have provided a safety valve for the discontents and fermentations of the popular mind, under real or supposed grievances, or under any occasions of dissatisfaction, by guaranteeing freedom of speech and of the press, the right of popular assemblies to declare and express the public will, and the right of petition and remonstrance addressed to the Government. The Constitution of the United States, on this point, reads thus: "Congress shall make no law abridging the freedom of speech, or of the press; or the right of the people peaceably to assemble, and to petition the Government for a redress of grievances."

The Constitution of the State of Pennsylvania has it thus: "The printing presses shall be free to every person who undertakes to examine the proceedings of the Legislature, or any branch of Government; and no law shall ever be made to restrain the right thereof. The free communication of thoughts and feelings is one of the invaluable rights of man; and every citizen may freely speak, write, and print on any subject, being responsible for the abuse of that liberty.... The citizens have a right, in a peaceable manner, to assemble together for their common good, and to apply to those invested with the powers of government for redress of grievances, or other proper purposes, by petition, address, or remonstrance."

We have selected the Constitution of Pennsylvania for what it says on this point, as it is more full than any other, and contains the substance of all. We believe, that this extract, in connexion with that from the National Constitution, comprehends the whole of the Constitutional law of the country on the subject, and that is a fair expression of the public mind—of the political creed of the citizens of the United States, in regard to the particulars here represented.

We observe, then, that certain *specific* modes of combined popular action for political purposes, are here licensed. Of course, we suppose it is fairly to be inferred, that the framers of these Constitutional laws did not intend to license *all* and *any* modes *whatever* of popular action for public purposes. Such an assumption would be preposterous and absurd. It would be tantamount to the setting aside of all authority, and the dissolution of *one* all government. On the contrary, the declaration, that *these* modes are lawful, is an implied and virtual declaration, that *other* modes are unlawful. We think there can be no mistake, and we trust, no difference of opinion, on this point. Because, if other mode be lawful, then *any* and *all* others are, and the rule falls to the ground—is good for nothing; it is, in that case, a mere mockery of legislation, and the community is left without law, and without government, in this particular.

Moreover, a consideration of the *occasion* of this law goes to settle the question of its meaning and limitation: It was the common and known prohibition of these rights, under absolute and despotic governments, and more particularly under the Colonial administration of British law in America, that suggested these declarations of rights in the establishment of our independence, and which caused them to be adopted as parts of Constitutional and fundamental law. These rights were deemed sufficient, and they have always proved satisfactory. They have also been held very sacred. The people of this country would shed their most precious blood, before they would surrender them. It was an invaluable acquisition to liberty. And as this law is deemed sufficient, and has proved so by experience, we suppose it will be allowed to be equally important, that it should not be *transcended*, as that it should be *maintained*; and that a licentious *extension* thereof is as criminal as an *abridgement*. It has every thing in it that a people can ask, who are free to choose their own legislators and magistrates. If the views of the public press, and the petitions and remonstrances of the people, carried forward to the Government, when they may see occasion for it, are not respected, the people know their remedy, and can effectually apply it at the polls. They have liberty of speech and of the press, the right of popular assemblages for the discussion of public interests and measures, and the right of petition, address, and remonstrance, guarantied to them; and to crown the whole, they are themselves the source of all law and government, always subjected to the will of the majority, in a Constitutional mode of action.

Now we ask, where is the license in the Constitutional law of this land for such a political machinery as the American Anti-Slavery Society? It cannot be found. Individuals are free to speak, write, and publish, what they please, on slavery, or any other subject—*they being responsible for the abuse of that liberty*. The people may assemble, *in a peaceable manner*, and discuss any subject that may be agreeable to them; they may pass any resolutions they may see fit, as an expression of their opinions or wishes; but the *only constitutional and lawful mode* of popular action for political purposes, designed to influence the measures of the Government, or to effect any change in the laws, apart from the use of the elective franchise, is for the people to connect themselves with the proper authorities, by petition, or address, or remonstrance, unless they see reasons for abandoning their purpose. There is no license for a *permanent* political organization, to act independently of the constituted authorities of the land; nor to act *with* them. Government requires no such auxilliary; much less can it tolerate an *opponent* of such a character. The Government is the *only* permanent, political organization, which the Constitution recognises.

We are inclined to believe, that these statements will commend themselves to the common sense of all intelligent persons, and that this position will be admitted as indisputable. What! an independent political body *within* the State, acting under a polity of its own, plotting and carrying on designs *against* the State, and claiming the State's protection, while it is enacting treason, if it chooses so to do! What an anomaly! Who ever dreamt that such a thing were possible? Who would think that it could be advocated and defended—maintained as a right? And yet, what else, and what less, is the American Anti-Slavery Society?

The wisdom of the Constitution, or Constitutions—for those of the States, and that of the nation, embody the same identical principles—in licensing such modes of political action as have been quoted, and in prohibiting all others, is obvious. If any association, or associations, of individuals, were at liberty to set up an independent political machinery, to be extended without limit, and to be managed without control or responsibility, there would be no safety for the constituted authorities of the States and Nation. They would be liable, at any time, to be undermined and overthrown by agencies under their own eyes. There is equal wisdom in prohibiting such combinations altogether; for there is no demand, there *can* be no lawful occasion, for them in such a government as ours, where the people can always move, without let or hinderance, directly, towards the objects they desire, or which the majority desire, under the prescribed forms of the Constitution and laws. If it were allowable for the people to depart from these forms in one instance, they might do it in another; if in one degree, they might extend it at their own option; and there would be no end to it. Sedition and treason, in that case, would be authorised by law. But, most happily, the Constitutional law of this land has been minutely scrupulous in prohibiting all permanent political organizations, which are not created by itself, as parts of one great political fabric, asserting *sole* empire over its own jurisdiction. We say, in *prohibiting* them, as we have before shown, that the license given is equally a law of prohibition for all that is not licensed.

This wisdom is moreover apparent from the consideration, that by adhering to these forms, there is always a balance of influence against any attempts to injure, or impair, or overthrow the Government, Constitution, and laws of the land, or to surprise the public by the advantages acquired by political combinations of a permanent and organized character. The freedom of speech guaranteed to one citizen, is guaranteed to all. Hence, the private influence of one man on one side, is balanced by that of another on the other side, of the same question; and between the two, the chances are in favour of the right. The same remark applies to the influence of the press: there is always a balance of power, operating on the public, so long as the forms of the Constitution are observed. In the same manner, popular assemblies of one party and the other, so long as they keep within the Constitutional license, neutralize each other, in all their inordinate excesses, and afford a chance for the right to prevail. Whenever a petition, or address, or remonstrance is preferred to Government, in regard to which there is a difference of opinion, its undue influence will be counteracted by another. And so a salutary balance of power is maintained in all the Constitutional modes of political action.

But the moment the Constitutional license is transcended, as in the case of the American Anti-Slavery Society, this healthful balance of power is lost. Such an unconstitutional organization steals a march upon the public, and by the amazing power of its vast political machinery, assails the Constitution and laws of the country, with no rival influence to counteract it. While the rest of the people keep *within* the laws, this combination has *transcended* them, and occupies the field of its usurpation alone. There is no balance of influence any where, that can lawfully be employed, except in the strong arm of authority. The public, the Government, the world, have been taken by surprise. Here is an immense and powerful combination, that has suddenly leaped from the sphere of the religious world, brought with it a machinery which was manufactured in that sphere, seized upon affairs of State, usurped the business of State, and neither the public, nor the Government, seem yet to know which end, or how, head or tail, to take hold of the monster. It comes in shapes unknown, unrecognized before, and has pounced upon the political fabric of the nation, with an apparent determination to rend it asunder, and tear it down before the eyes of the world. Like as Satan, when he came with errand fatal to our race, from out Hell's regions, and approached the gates that opened from that dark abyss, encountered and addressed his monster child, so the Government, not less amazed, seems also to say to this unexpected Apparition:

> "Whence, and what art thou, execrable shape,
> That durst, though grim and terrible, advance
> Thy miscreated front athwart my way?"

But, we fear, that a like truce will not be made between these parties. Like as "Sin" gave her own history to her Father, so the world may yet be favoured with a philosophical account of this other monster, a part of which, peradventure, shall be found in these pages.

It is the perfectly anomalous character and position of the American Anti-Slavery Society, that has so embarrassed and overwhelmed the public mind, produced such a vast excitement, and frightened half the nation. Armed with a machinery hitherto unknown in the political world, it has broken through the bounds of law and the restraints of the Constitution, opened its artillery on both these departments of our political fabric, and so astounded the public, that few have yet learned how this audacious assault has been planned and executed, or what is the character of the enemy to be encountered. It is because, in this political crusade, the actors have thoroughly transcended the prescribed limits of Constitutional action, and entered a field untrodden before, in an unknown shape, that the public know not where to find them, or how to meet and take hold of them. The battle, hitherto, has been all their own; and it cannot be denied, that they have done execution, and stand responsible for infinite mischief. Neither is it any less certain, in our opinion, that, with all the advantage and power of their organization, if it should be recognized as lawful, and permitted by the public authorities of our country to go on, without check or control, they will revolutionize the Government, and divide the Union. All beyond this is uncertain, and fearfully so.

Suppose the Abolitionists had kept within the bounds of law, and contented themselves with that freedom of speech and of the press, with such public discussions, and with such petitions, addresses, and remonstrances to Government, as the Constitution authorises; suppose they had been as mild and Christian-like in their action on this subject, as the Quakers; their influence would then have distilled like the dew, fallen like the rain, and cheered the heart like the sun. In such a case, the subject could still have been discussed with reason and temperance, throughout the wide community, not excepting even the South; the South would not have been alarmed; the free colored population would not have been, as now, filled with all bitterness and malice; the amelioration of the condition of slaves would have continued and increased, as before, instead of that augmented rigour of discipline and surveillance to which the South has been compelled by these violent measures; the country would have remained in peace, and the whole subject would still have been open to free and candid discussion every where, and with every body. Whereas, the erection of this unconstitutional machinery, and the spirit with which it has been swayed, has put the whole Republic out of temper, and out of joint; has made pro-slavery men of one party, and fanatics of another; has unfitted the colored population, free and bond, for the culture of benevolence; has rivetted the chains of slavery with tenfold power, blighted the prospects, and thrown forward the period, of ultimate emancipation, for a time which baffles prophecy, unless, peradventure—which God forbid—this movement shall prevail to break down the Government, and let loose the spirit of fiends to desolate the land. The strife henceforth will be, not that of benevolence for the good of the slave—for the Abolitionists themselves are his most dangerous foes—but it will be between this organized sedition and the Government of the country—between the Constitution and a grand political faction. And all this as the consequence of departing from the wholesome regulations of law, of setting up a romantic sympathy as a substitute for true benevolence, and fanaticism for Christianity.

In view of the argument of this chapter, we trust we shall stand justified with all reasonable minds, for the heading we have placed over it, and for the title of the book. It has been from a conscientious conviction of the seditious character of the American Anti-slavery Society, that we have sat down to this task. The public generally have felt, that this association was warring against the supreme law of the land; but nobody has taken pains to set forth the argument by which it is proved. Every body has seen, that the tranquillity of the country has been disturbed, and a dissolution of the Union threatened, by the action of this Society; but the more common impression has been, that it is rather the result of rashness and imprudence, than the effect of an unlawful political combination. The popular disgust and indignation, with which some of the more outrageous proceedings of Abolitionists have been received, have arisen from a vague and undefined notion, that they were wrong—and wrong in relation to the Constitution and laws of the land; but, we think, that the true position, and proper political character of this Society, as being seditious, has not generally been perceived. If, indeed, we are right in the views here presented, we hope they may be the means of enlightening the public. Abolitionists themselves, especially the most active and determined, we have little hope of benefitting; else, we might have studied more to humour their prejudices, and gain them over to reason. We have rather been convinced, that the greatness and danger of the error demand a somewhat decided and vigorous treatment. We have observed with pain, that the people of the South are getting more and more into the feeling and conviction, that a dissolution of the Union will be necessary for their own protection. In so far, therefore, as the people of the North would deprecate such a result, it is most desirable, that they should thoroughly understand the position and character of the Abolition organization, in order that they may be prepared to appreciate and treat it according to its merits. If, indeed, it is a sedition, and can be clearly proved to be such, to the satisfaction of the public, can it be supposed, that it would continue to have the same moral power, even with its own advocates? Will not many of them shrink from the thought of being traitors to their country; and more especially when they shall have occasion to see, as by this time they ought to see, that, in such a course, they are rivetting, instead of breaking, the chains of slavery, unless they succeed in plunging the nation into a civil war, which ought to be still more revolting to their feelings? How much more should such a conviction arm that portion of the Northern public, who have never fallen into this delusion, with zeal and determination to vindicate the honor of their country, and maintain its laws, not, indeed, by a persecution of those who have been led astray, but by showing, in all suitable ways, their unyielding attachment to the Constitution and Government, in its unavoidable struggle against such an unlawful combination, and by convincing the people of the South, that there is a sympathy in the North, that will not abandon them in the trying and perilous condition, into which they have been thrown by this seditious movement?

And would we advise an authoritative suppression of this sedition? We say not, that we would. Ours is a Government of forbearance, because it is the Government of the people. As we have reason to suppose, that the public generally have not even yet discovered the true position of the Anti-slavery Society, in relation to the Constitution, much less can we presume to say, that the members of that Society, as a body, have ever imagined, that they were involved in the responsibility of seditious action against the Government of their country. We charitably believe, that for the most part, their benevolent sympathies have been worked upon by the exaggerated statements and high colored pictures of more artful, of ambitious, and less innocent men; and that, when left to choose between sedition and the Union, they will unhesitatingly prefer the latter, even though the former, if it had been a lawful enterprise, might still seem to them a worthy and desirable object. But, if the extremity must unavoidably come, to dissolve the Union and the Government, or encounter this movement by the strong arm of authority, with our present views of its seditious character, we cannot entertain a doubt, on which side it would be our duty to engage. Nevertheless, our confidence in the good sense of the people, leads us to hope for better things.

CHAPTER III
THE SEDITIOUS CHARACTER OF THE ANNUAL REPORT OF THE AMERICAN ANTI-SLAVERY SOCIETY OF 1838

If the showing already made, in regard to the seditious *organization* of the American Anti-slavery Society, be a fair one, its action as such becomes a conspiracy in the Republic, so far as it militates against its political fabric. It is no more than fair to notice, that in the first article of the Constitution of this Society, it is assumed, that "slavery is contrary to the principles of *our* republican form of government." This is a very material point, vital, fundamental, so far as it relates to the question now in hand. The truth of this assumption would justify the *cause*, in which this Society are engaged, so long as it should be sustained in a Constitutional way; though it cannot justify an independent political organization in the Republic for such an object. We have already pointed out, as we trust clearly, the only Constitutional modes of political action for reform, or any other purposes, under the Government; and shown that this Society is unconstitutional. The truth of this assumption, therefore, would not justify its mode of action, and it would still be open to the charge of sedition. But, let us see, whether this assumption be true.

"Slavery is contrary to the principles of *our* republican form of government." If they mean to say, it is contrary to the principles of the free States, as recognised and established for their own separate jurisdictions, it is true. But it was quite unnecessary to say it, as all the world knew it before. If they mean to say it is contrary to the principles of a republican form of government in the *abstract*, as a *theory*, it may be true, or it may be false, and depends entirely upon the character of the theory that is set up. This is a question, which cannot easily be settled, because it is a matter of *opinion*, not of *fact*. The people of the South would be on one side, and those of the North on the other; and we ourself, be it known, should be on the side of the North. If the question be as to the *common* opinion, prevalent among mankind, of the principles of a republican form of government, this Society is doubtless right on *that* ground. But we apprehend, indeed we know, and every body knows, that it is not a question of opinion, but of fact, that is involved in this assumption. Did the Society mean to say, that "slavery is contrary to the principles" of the Slave-holding States? Manifestly not. What, then, did they mean? Contrary to the principles of the Government of the United States, undoubtedly. "Slavery is contrary to the principles of *our* Republican form of Government." We say, then, that as a *fact*, this is *false*; and we need travel no further to prove it, than from the Preamble of the Constitution of this Society, in which this assertion is made, to the second Article, where we find this clause: "While it (the Society) admits, that each State, in which slavery exists, has the *exclusive* right, *by the Constitution of the United States*, to legislate in regard to its Abolition in said State," &c. As this is a candid recognition of that part, and of those "*principles* of *our* Republican form of Government," which we shall have occasion in another place to introduce in form, it is superfluous to quote the passages here, inasmuch as this Society, by its own confession, has done the work *for* us, and *against* itself. It is a simple question of *fact*; and that fact recognized, in express terms, by the Society, in the second article of its own Constitution, the assumption of the Preamble, in regard to this point, is proved to be *false*. Slavery, therefore, is *not* contrary to the principles of *our* Republican form of Government; and the Constitution of the United States, (Art. II. Sec. 2d. Clause 3d.) which we shall hereafter consider, recognises the *validity* of property in the Slave, and engages to defend it throughout the Union; and it is well known, that, by the force of this law, runaway Slaves are habitually recovered. It will be understood, that we are not discussing the propriety of this law, but the fact. It is a "*principle* of *our* Republican form of Government;" and as would seem, a potent and paramount one.

All the other principles of the American Anti-Slavery Society will avail nothing, *politically considered*, so long as they are false in this. They have hazarded their whole cause, in an open and seditious conflict with the Government of the United States, *on a false assumption as to fact*!

We shall now proceed to a consideration of the seditious character of the Annual Report of this Society, of 1838. This Society must now be viewed, as we have proved it to be, in the light of a grand and independent political organization, set up in the Republic, and at war with it—as an unconstitutional and self-erected corporation. Any political action it may assume, therefore, whether *for* or *against* the Republic, is unconstitutional. The Government wants not its help—certainly it has never asked for it— much less can it tolerate a conspiracy. What may be lawful for a private citizen to do, is unlawful for this Society as a political organization of its specific character. What may be lawful for popular assemblies, or associations, acting in the modes prescribed by the Constitution, for political ends, of whatever nature, is unlawful for this Society, because it is a body unknown to the Constitution and laws of the land. It is a State *within* the State, that has asked no leave to be, that is prohibited by law, acting under a State machinery, disturbing the peace of the State, and threatening its overthrow.

The Annual Report of this Society of 1838, is a document of a remarkable character, when viewed in this light. It is almost exclusively political. It seems true enough, as its own language declares, that "abolitionism *must* have much to do with politics." It discusses all the affairs of the nation, and of the States, in relation to this great and portentous subject, as must be confessed with no inconsiderable ability, and with a boldness which might astound any one who looks at the position which this Society occupies, and the sweep of its influence; and more especially, when we consider the decorum, and the gravity, and the solemnity which, one would think, ought to characterize such a document, emanating from so great a body, on such an occasion, and so exciting a theme, when every opportunity for reflexion had been afforded, and when there could be little apology for violence of language, or uncourteous demeanor, towards public men, and the public authorities. Even if the existence and action of this Society had been constitutional and lawful, as it was no doubt thought to be by its members, still there was something in the elevation and responsibility of its position before the public, on account of which the ordinary proprieties, which might seem to be reasonably incumbent on all such bodies, had strong claims to be respected. In all seriousness, we do not think the time has come—certainly we hope not—when the political violence and rancour of newspaper columns, can be regarded as becoming in such a document. Could it easily be believed, by those who have not read this Report—a document occupying one hundred and fifty-two crowded octavo pages, the major part of which breathes the same spirit—that all public men, from the President of the United States downwards, including Senators, Governors, Ministers to foreign nations, Magistrates, and officers of every grade, of the States and Nation, who may have manifested any symptoms of opposition to Abolitionism, or whose public acts have been unfavorable to it, are treated as if —— but we will not trust ourselves to describe it, lest we fall into the same excess of rudeness.

Freedom of speech, and of the press, in treating of public men and public measures, is undoubtedly guaranteed by the Constitutional law of this land; and if this Report had emanated from an authorised and constitutional body, no legal exception could have been taken to its character or terms, however it might seem to be indecorous and undignified, not to say inflammatory and incendiary. In point of dignity, as being the public and solemn act of such a body, we think there could be but one opinion of its character. As if the genius that presided over its composition were not prolific enough in nerve astounding artillery, it seems to have taken out a license to cater from the widest range of Newspaper authorities, and ex parte statements and reports, for its facts and arguments, and for its delicious treat of suavity and kindness.

But there is yet a more portentous aspect of this Report, that remains to be considered. We allude to its treatment of the decisions of the highest Legislative Assembly of the Nation: the Senate and House of Representatives of the United States.

It is well known, that the disposal made in Congress of petitions on the subject of Abolition, has not been agreeable to the members of this Society, although it might be difficult to see how it could have been done very differently, so long as the majority of both Houses were opposed to the object; unless it be claimed as a right to occupy the whole time of the National Legislature, in reading and discussing these petitions, to the neglect of all other business, which would seem to be very unreasonable. No new idea could be presented; the mind of Congress was made up; and it would seem to be factious to demand a separate consideration of every petition on this subject, without any prospect or hope of a different result. So far from involving a denial of the right of petition, any other course would have been a manifest violation of public duty, in neglecting the ordinary and other affairs of legislation. The wishes of these petitioners being known, the design of the Constitution in regard to such a matter was answered; and so long as they were known to be a very small minority of the nation, and the great majority opposed, no action on the subject, in the way of legislation, could be expected. It would be altogether unreasonable, and "contrary to the principles of our republican form of Government." Moreover, the great majority of both houses of Congress considered it, not only disturbing, but unconstitutional, either for them, as a branch of the Government, or for the people, not citizens of the Slave States, to meddle with the subject, with a view to legislation, as these petitions requested. Of course, no farther action could be expected, in that quarter, till the use of the elective franchise might carry into Congress a set of men of a different opinion.

Not to speak particularly of the charges of violating the Constitution, thrown upon the House of Representatives, by this Report; or of its "seditious members," as it calls them; or of the "demoniac yells," by which the remonstrance of the Ex-President Adams was silenced; it is more to our present purpose to call attention to the treatment rendered to the Senate, in this same document, for the resolutions passed in that body on this subject, in January, 1838: —

"Neither humanity, nor patriotism, will permit us to pass over this proceeding of the Senate, without setting it in what seems to us its true light. *We pronounce it a bootless usurpation — an act equally unconstitutional and impotent.* If these expressions should seem disrespectful towards the highest branch of the National Legislature, let it be remembered, that that officially august body can claim to be respected only while it respects the primary act of the people, by virtue of which it exists. *When it oversteps the limits of the Constitution*, for any object whatever, *its authority is forfeited.* But when it oversteps those limits for the attainment of an object which is in itself essentially absurd and impossible — when it essays to do by mere resolutions what it would be ridiculous to attempt by statutory enactment — *it must sink to the level of contempt....* If we are correct in these views of the nature and force of our Federal Constitution, the Senate of the United States was employed from the 3d to the 13th of January, 1838, *in enacting a farce well adapted to turn legislation into mockery.*"

Not to speak of the *exceeding indecorum* of this language, as coming from what ought to be a *reverend*, as it is doubtless a *religious* as well as a political body, it is certainly going quite far enough for a power, whose lawful existence and action for any such purposes, hang suspended at best in a doubtful balance. It falls on the ear like the death sounding knell of revolutionary times. But we cannot consider it doubtful, in view of the facts and reasonings heretofore brought under review, whether this Society be a lawful one, or not. Our own convictions compel us to "pronounce it," not simply "a bootless," but *seditious* "usurpation."

Here, then, is a grand and permanent political organization, self-erected, self-governed, independent, and irresponsible, having no connexion with the Government of the country, but yet usurping the business of that Government; having come into existence, and set up its action, in violation of the prescribed forms of the Constitution; with a distinct and systematic polity of its own creation, on a scale comparing with the machinery of a State; with a President and seventeen Vice Presidents; four Secretaries, one for correspondence with lecturing agents scattered over the country, and for other general purposes; one for correspondence with foreign countries; one devoted to domestic political action and financial agents; and one to record the doings of the Society; a Treasurer; a Board of one hundred and three Managers; 1350 auxiliaries, 13 of which are on the grand scale of State Societies; 38 travelling agents, and 75 circulating within a narrower compass; disbursing an annual income of $50,000, besides a vast amount of gratuitous labour; employing the power of the press to the amount of 646,502 copies of various literary productions annually distributed; and all these various forms of political and combined power constantly augmenting. Such is the machinery of this institution—and such the history of its origin,—an institution, which, in its annual assemblage, by representation from all its dependencies, dares, by its own public, recorded, and proclaimed acts, to "pronounce" the solemn decisions of the Senate of the nation "*an unconstitutional usurpation*," and to declare its "*authority forfeited!*"—thus unfurling the flag of rebellion, and like the Jacobins of revolutionary France, seeming to say to the swelling of its train—Onward! Such a power legalized, with no balance of influence to counteract it, with all the advantages of its organization, of its peculiar and effective modes of operation, is enough to revolutionize any State, and any nation.

CHAPTER IV
THE SEDITIOUS CHARACTER OF
THE AMERICAN ANTI-SLAVERY
SOCIETY FARTHER CONSIDERED

Having proved the sedition of the American Anti-Slavery Society as a political organization, which has usurped the business of the Government, under a form prohibited by the Constitution, which of course involves two points of criminality, we shall now proceed to show, that it is seditious in another important and grave particular, as having committed, and as continuing to commit, a trespass on the political rights of the slave-holding States, as guaranteed to them by the Federal Compact, and as recognized by the law of nations.

In the first place, the action of this Society, as a grand political organization, on the social fabric of foreign States—for the slave States are foreign in respect to it—with the intent to change it against their consent, and thus disturbing their domestic tranquility, is a violation of the law of nations. This is sedition in a higher and more important sense, than any combined assault on the social institutions of a community by its own members, inasmuch as the remedy is more difficult to be attained, and more momentous in its consequences. It can be settled only by the sword. The noninterference of one nation in the domestic condition of another, is an established doctrine, and a settled maxim, of international law. A trespass on this principle is always considered tantamount to a declaration of war. Just in proportion as the peace of nations, in their relations to each other, is more important than the domestic tranquility of a single State, and the breach of it more difficult to be healed, is the criminality of such trespass increased. The action of the American Anti-Slavery Society, therefore, on the slave-holding States, as an interference of this kind, is much more responsible and more criminal, than as a violation of the social fabric of the United States. It matters not what may be the faults in the social condition of any State or nation, in the judgment and conscience of the people of another State or nation; such considerations, however aggravated and serious, furnish no ground or justification for interference; but the fact of interference is war begun.

The American Anti-Slavery Society, as we have seen, is a political organization—unlawful, indeed, but yet such is its character—and as such they have great power. They hold in their hands the peace and well being of all the slave States. On the principle above recognized—the soundness of which we dare to say will not be questioned—its action on those States is war. It is impossible that this Society should screen itself from this responsibility under the plea, that they are only using that freedom of speech and of the press, and other modes of social influence, which the Constitutional law of the land has guaranteed. For we have shown, that in the machinery they have set up, and in their modes of action, they have transcended that law; and as a consequence it will follow, that they have cast themselves beyond its protection. It will, moreover, be vain for them to plead, that they are a part of the same nation, and that however it may appear, that they have been guilty of sedition in disturbing the tranquility, by violating the laws, of the Federal Commonwealth, they have not trespassed on the law of nations. For, we shall yet, and very soon, have occasion to see, that the sovereignty of the States composing the American Union, is perfect and unimpaired, in all that has not been resigned or prohibited in the Federal Constitution for national purposes; and that, with these exceptions, the several States occupy precisely the same position, in their relations to each other, as do any other States or nations. And the institution of slavery is not comprehended in these exceptions, but remains the sovereign right of the States where it is established, so far as it concerns other States, and other nations, and so far as concerns the whole world out of their jurisdiction. It is therefore true, that the American Anti-Slavery Society, being a political body, incorporated in its own claimed and independent right, has made war on the slave-holding States of the Union.

But as it happens, this Society is a nondescript organization, because it is an unlawful one. It has no territorial jurisdiction, and no political relations, apart from its own constituent elements; it is a parvenu and stranger among recognised republics and nations—a mere pirate, a brigand, that has broken loose from law, and invaded, from inaccessible ambushes, the peace of whole communities, putting in peril the lives of their citizens, and their institutions. It cannot, therefore, be approached by the injured parties, under that *lex talionis* of nations, which is customarily resorted to, when their honor has been insulted, their rights violated, or their interests impaired, by a foreign foe. This Society protects itself under the shield of that Government, of the laws of which its very existence is a violation. That Government, therefore, is responsible for its action, and the injured parties have a claim upon it for indemnification and redress of the evils which they suffer. In existing circumstances, this is the only medium by which a remedy can be obtained. Nevertheless, the law of nations has been violated by foreign interference in the domestic condition of the slaveholding States—an interference, which, in any other case, would be regarded as a just occasion for retaliation by a resort to arms.

In the discussion of this point of the subject, we have nothing to do with the rights of the slave in relation to the authorities by which he is held in bondage, any more than with those of the serfs of Poland, or of Hungary, or of Prussia, in case the sympathies of this Society should happen to take that direction, and make war on the peace and social institutions of those countries. The two cases are precisely parallel, and one is as justifiable as the other, by the law of nations, and of human society as it exists. The authorities of those countries would fairly hold the Government of the United States responsible for such an invasion, in the same manner, as we are bound by treaty with the British Government to maintain our obligations of neutrality on the Canadian frontier, and to prevent our citizens from invading the rights, and destroying the lives of British subjects in their own territory. Even though it could be shown, that the Canadians are oppressed, and deprived of their just rights, still it would be no justification or apology for the interference of our citizens. The same principle precisely applies to the action of the American Anti-Slavery Society on the Southern States.

But this Society is even more criminal than these invaders of Canada, because it has first violated the laws of the United States by the erection of a systematic and unlawful polity, an unconstitutional and powerful machinery, the plans and scope of which, if not abandoned or suppressed, are adequate to protract, perpetuate, and forever to augment the illegal and destructive powers they have set in operation, till they shall upset the Government, and desolate the South; whereas the invasion of Canada is nothing more than the mad enterprise of a few deluded individuals. Had they followed the example of the American Anti-Slavery Society,—which, doubtless, they had an equal right to do—and set up a like political organization, under like immunities, and with like strength of preparation, they would inevitably have involved this country in a war with Great Britain. What sufferance, therefore, has been practised towards this Society! And what protracted injuries have the Southern States been compelled to endure!

As remarked in the previous chapter, it is the perfectly anomalous character of this enterprise, which has so long embarrassed the public mind. All not engaged in it, have felt it to be wrong; the wide spread indignation, and the popular outbreaks it has occasioned in rebuke of its designs and operations, show that it involves some great and vitally important principle in our social fabric; but its distinct and definite character, and its exact political position and relations, have not heretofore been evolved and so exhibited, as to enable the public to see it clearly, and to know how to treat it. It was the suddenness and novelty of the movement, as a grand and unlawful political transaction, that astounded the public mind, and threw it from the balance of its wonted composure; but the agitation and disturbance it occasioned are prima facie evidence of its aberration from right principles—of its criminality. That cannot be regarded, by sober minds, other than a highly responsible operation in society, which breaks its peace, and puts in peril its political existence; and we dare to aver, that the common impression of its criminality cannot be without good reason. Even if no law had been violated, other than a common and implied obligation of all good citizens to keep the peace, and sustain the tranquil operation of our Constitution and laws, that is enough to authorize a verdict of guilty against this Society on the *general* charge of a public nuisance. But in all points of view we find there is recognised and written law for the case, and the common feeling of the public mind is honored and sustained by the investigation. We might fairly presume it impossible for this feeling to be wrong, as it springs up spontaneously in the bosom of a community where slavery is not only disapproved, but abhorred.

It is morally certain, therefore, that it is not a feeling of complacency in slavery, nor any desire, nor even willingness, to see it perpetuated, that has arrayed itself so generally in the North against the Abolition movement. But it is a conviction, that the supreme law of the land has been invaded, and the certain knowledge, that the public peace has been disturbed, and the stability and permanence of our social and political institutions put in peril. It is a correct view of the nature of our political fabric, which leads the public mind, in such an exigency, to the conclusion, that the people of one State have no right to interfere with the domestic condition of another, unless that right has been *specified* and conferred in the Federal compact; and that even then, it can be employed only in general concert by a representation of all the States in Congress assembled. The people know, as they are bound to know, so long as they claim the privilege of self-government, that the rights of the several States, not transferred or prohibited by the general Constitution, are sacred in their own keeping, and ought to be sacred from foreign interference and invasion. And although they may not have discovered, and as would appear, have not, as a body, that the *organization* of the American Anti-Slavery is an open and flagrant violation of law, yet they have felt and been convinced, that its *transactions* are of this character. Hence the public feeling of remonstrance and indignation, that has been manifested. It is not unprovoked and wanton; it is not an opposition to the principle of Abolition in itself considered, for all the early and abiding prejudices of the North are on that side; it is not persecution, however such a clamour may be raised, for there is no adequate moral cause; but it is an attachment to the existing, and long tried, institutions of the country, which, though they may not be perfect, are yet deemed too valuable to be suddenly and ruthlessly broken down by a faction—by an organized sedition. This feeling, therefore, is worthy of some respect—nay, of the greatest respect—for it proves to be based on sound Constitutional principles. We hold it to be impossible, that a lawful enterprise could produce so great an excitement, under a Constitution and Government so good, and so well approved, as ours.

But, having disposed of this subject, as a violation of the law of nations, which involves the highest criminality, because it is liable to work mischief on the largest scale, and of the deepest die, let us consider it as a violation of the Federal Compact, in an Article not yet introduced: "The powers not delegated to the United States by the Constitution, nor prohibited by it to the States, are reserved to the States respectively, or to the people." This is the Tenth Article of the Constitution of the United States; and although it involves precisely the same principle of international law, as that we have just been considering, it presents itself here in the character and with the sanction of a corporate element of our own political fabric. It draws the line, in black and white, between the powers of the nation and those of the States respectively. It leaves the States in absolute and uncontrolled possession of all the sovereign powers, customarily asserted and employed by sovereign States, which are not delegated or prohibited in the general Constitution; and one of those powers is a sovereign right of legislation and control over the institution of slavery. Another, of course, is the common and national right, universally recognized, of claiming the unrestricted scope and benefit of the law of noninterference in regard to this matter. This Article of the Federal Constitution places every State precisely on the footing, and in the position, of nations entirely independent of each other, in all particulars not surrendered or prohibited by this instrument. Its language is, that all other powers—"the powers not delegated, &c. are *reserved* to the States *respectively*, or to the people." Whatever may have been intended by this alternative of "*the people*," it cannot be construed to qualify or restrict the object of our present remarks. We suppose it points to the principle of general sovereignty, as appears to be recognized in the Ninth Article, as follows: "The enumeration, in the Constitution, of certain rights, shall not be construed to deny or disparage others retained by the people;" that is—if we may be allowed the privilege of interpretation here—those general rights of sovereignty, which belong to all nations, acting in their Constitutional modes, authorizing measures adapted to unforeseen exigencies. Certainly, this rule cannot be construed to authorize a minority, or a faction, to do what they please, or to depart from the constituted forms of law. And that is all the bar we have any occasion, for our present purpose, to introduce, whatever other interpretation may be given to it.

The sovereignty of the States, in and over their own respective jurisdictions, in all that is not taken out of their hands by the National Constitution, is recognized and settled by the Tenth Article; and the power to claim the privilege of *noninterference* from foreign quarters, as to their domestic condition, is a part of that sovereignty. Consequently, if the people, or any association of people, in one State, should interfere with the domestic concerns of another, they are guilty of sedition in and against the Republic; and on the principles of international law, if it be a seriously disturbing movement—of which the injured party is constituted judge—they have made war upon that State, and furnished a just occasion of resort to arms, if remedy and redress can be obtained in no other way. We speak not the language of advice, but of the law simply—of recognized and established principles of civilized and political society;—and so far as the question of sedition is concerned, we speak of the supreme law of this land. In the condition and relations of the members of our Confederacy, the remedy for such interference is doubtless to be sought through the medium, and by the action, of the General Government. If that Government should prove incompetent, or be unwilling, to perform the duty claimed by the injured party, and devolving upon it in such an exigency, the natural consequence would be a dissolution of the Union, and a probable resort to arms. And this is the result to which our country is now imminently exposed by the seditious and criminal interferences of the American Anti-Slavery Society, with the domestic condition of the slave-holding States. They have no more right to meddle with Southern slavery, than with that of the Irish peasantry, or of the miserable beings immured in British Manufactories, or of Hungarian, or Polish, or Russian boors, which, in each of these instances, is far more worthy of commiseration and relief, than the slavery of the Southern States, and calls louder for the offices of humanity, if any such interferences would be tolerated.

But the case is even stronger than has yet been stated. The General Government itself cannot interfere in this matter, except to keep the peace, and *prevent* interference; and this they are bound to do. The Federal Constitution has recognized the validity of slave property, and established a law to maintain and defend it, throughout the jurisdiction of the United

States, as follows: "No person held to service, or labor, in one State, under the laws thereof, escaping to another, shall in consequence of any law or regulation therein, be discharged from such service, or labor; but shall be delivered up on claim of the party to whom such labor or service may be due." Art. IV, Sect. II, Clause 3d. The Tenth Article of the Constitution cuts off all interference of the General Government, in the matter of slavery, as it exists in any of the States. Next, it debars interference to all the States, in relation to each other. Much more does it debar such interference to private citizens, or to any combinations of citizens, in any State, or States, with the slavery of other States. For, surely, that right of property, which the public authorities may not infringe, may not be infringed by those who are not invested with authority. Neither can a private citizen, or any combinations of citizens, lawfully disturb or weaken the possession of property, which is sanctioned and upheld by the laws of the land.

Moreover, the General Government is bound by an express law of the Federal Constitution to protect and defend this species of property against invasion, conspiracy, insurrection, and violence: "The United States shall protect every State in this Union *against invasion*; and on application of the legislature, or of the executive, when the legislature cannot be convened, *against domestic violence*." Of course, this is a general and comprehensive rule for all possible exigencies of the kind; but it is generally understood — the last clause, particularly, respecting "domestic violence" — to have been enacted in anticipation of *servile* insurrections, and such other disturbances as are liable to occur under a system of slavery. Any how, the rule applies to these cases, and comprehends them; and that is enough. The General Government is bound to keep the peace under its own laws; and whenever the slave-holding States shall have occasion for its services, in consequence of "domestic violence," or of "invasion," they have a right to demand them, under this law of the Constitution; and they would no doubt be promptly afforded.

We see, therefore, that slavery is protected and defended at all points by the political fabric of this country. We profess, that we have no complacency in slavery, and never had: and that we have no gratification in coming to this conclusion, so far as it presents the prospect of the perpetuity of this acknowledged evil. But the time has come when a far greater evil, than that of slavery, threatens this land, in the unlawful measures which have been concerted, and which are being unlawfully urged, to do it away. The time has come, when it is important for the public to know what the law is, in relation to this movement; that they may know how to appreciate it, and how to act. The time has come, when it would be treason to the country wilfully to conceal the law, or to misinterpret it; for the law is the only power, that can settle this question in the public mind, on this side of that fearful resort, which brings despotism first, and barbarism last. Whatever the law is, we want to know it; the people of this country want to know it; and we believe they will abide by it, till, in peaceable times, they can make a better, if a better can be made.

The Abolitionists of this country are fast driving the people to the law — to a law, which has long been asleep and forgotten, because there was no demand for its authority; to a law, which we think, will assuredly work against the Agitators; to a law, which may yet have occasion to say to the tempest they have raised — "Hitherto shalt thou come, but no further."

CHAPTER V
VIOLENT REFORMS, AND THEIR CONNEXION WITH ABOLITIONISM

It can hardly have escaped the attentive observer of the history of our country, that for a considerable period, and to a great extent, it has been characterised by *violent reforms*, both in religion and morals; and it would be impossible, in our judgment, to understand the causes of the Abolition movement, if we should leave out of view this important and prominent historical feature. All great movements in society have their moral causes, and it is by referring to them, that we are enabled to ascertain their true character.

Religion has always been a potent element in American society, and it is to the conservative power of Christianity, that we owe our greatest blessings. But it does not remain for us to prove what history has decided, that religion may be abused and perverted. In such a case, it becomes important to distinguish between Christianity and religious excesses, or corruptions, and to rescue the former from a responsibility which would dishonor and injure it. When religion is profaned and degraded by extravagant modes of action; when it becomes rude and violent, instead of maintaining the genuine character of Christian suavity and mildness; when it assumes an overbearing and despotic dictation to private and public conscience, instead of the kind and winning arts of persuasion, which shine so conspicuously in the example of the Divine founder of Christianity, and of his Apostles;—and more especially, when it has leaped from its appropriate sphere of the moral, to the agitations of the political, world, seized on a stupendous political machinery in violation of the laws of the country, disturbed civil order to an alarming extent, threatened to overthrow the Government, and to deluge the land in the blood of a civil war—it is time to enquire into the causes of such a movement, how it originated, and how it may be checked, if checked it can be. These causes cannot be understood, without alluding to the facts and events of our religious history; for it is after all, and in truth, a religious movement, even by its own public and authoritative confession, as before seen. The Constitutional law of this land has carefully excluded religion from a participation in the authorities of State, and it cannot lawfully meddle with its affairs. It is a notable fact, however, notwithstanding these cautious provisions, that it has finally and suddenly overstepped these constitutional barriers, and usurped the most important and most momentous State questions, that could possibly be taken in hand.

In the first place, we remark, as a simple matter of fact—the deductions from which will afterwards claim our attention—that certain very extraordinary and painful scenes, sufficiently well known, have been enacted in our religious history, bordering on fanaticism, in some of the means employed, and modes adopted, for the extension of the interests of religion, according to the particular views of those engaged in these measures. So long, however, as those excesses were confined to religious action, they have been tolerated and protected by the laws of the land. It is the spirit of our Government, and the general temper of the community, not to disturb religion, even when its measures, in the judgment of the more sober, are deemed very extravagant and fanatical. Hence the rather *forcing* methods that have been so extensively adopted to gain and multiply converts, have been connived at, because they have been allowed to be sincere, and it was hoped they might be useful, as a conscientiously religious man is a better citizen than one whose sense of moral obligation is not founded in religious motives. This high stimulation of the moral world, however, has had the effect to produce an extensive and powerfully active leaven of a specific character, which seemed to require a wider scope of action, or an action the results of which might be somewhat more palpable in the common regions of society, than that which relates merely to the spiritual affections of mankind. In a word, instead of being satisfied with the religion of those "who declare plainly, that they *seek* a country" not yet possessed, it has shown a disposition to take under its charge a country *already* possessed. A religious faith, which ought to have maintained ulterior and higher aims, has degenerated somewhat into a religious patriotism; which still might have been well enough, as to any objections from general society, if it had not transcended the laws of the land. But it was perfectly natural, that a spirit which was violent, and addicted to forcing measures in one department of society, should also be violent, and employ like forcing measures in another, whenever its drift or inclinations should tempt it from its original and legitimate sphere of action.

It will be understood, of course, that we allude, in the first place, to the violence which has been so extensively manifested in religious reforms; and next, to the same spirit which afterwards took hold of Abolitionism. It was the breaking over of all religious order in the first instance, which prepared the way for the violation of civil order in the second. That boldness which trampled on custom in one case, was naturally schooled to set at defiance the law in the other.

But all breaches of propriety and of law, human or divine, are generally a work of degrees. Moral reforms came next to the religious—to neither of which, of course, do we take exception, any farther than as respects the violence that has been practised. But it is equally known, that the excesses which characterized one class, have been carried into the other. That religious patriotism, if we may call it so—an honorable appellation, certainly—which began to trouble itself with the condition and affairs of the country, soon discovered, that the state of public and general morals required attention—a conclusion most natural and most worthy, and an object which could hardly fail to meet with general approbation. And accordingly it has been approved, and well sustained. It was a work, in its various forms, from which much good was expected, and by which, no doubt, much good has been done.

But, unfortunately, the same excesses and the same violence, which characterized the religious operations of the country so extensively, were transferred into the moral reforms which were undertaken, and became a principal ingredient, because it happened, that the most violent religionists had a principal hand and a controlling influence in these matters also. As in religion, they undertook to convert sinners by force, so they undertook to reclaim mankind from their vices by force; and as they had adopted various new inventions and machineries for the former operations, so they did for the latter. But *force* was the dominant power in all—forcing opinions, forcing conscience, forcing the will—in the one case fulminating the terrors which come up from the future world to frighten mankind into religion; and in the other, arming themselves with all the power of an associated influence to destroy the characters of those who differed from them in opinion, as to the best modes of moral reformation, or who did not fall in with all their extravagant and coercing measures. The sanctuary of domestic and private life was not secure from their invasion; the thunders of authoritative anathemas pealed on the ears of the public, from the solemn decisions of imposing popular Conventions, to proscribe opposition and remonstrance, because it was *assumed* to be wrong and criminal, by a judgment *ex cathedra*; the title was claimed to examine every private citizen as to his private habits and opinions, and to denounce him, if heterodox; nor did they wait even for that; for they had the sagacity to discover what a man was by looking in his face. The character of no man was safe under such an inquisitorial, all pervading, self-constituted, and irresponsible tribunal, if he did not succumb at once to its authority.

Violent *moral* reforms constituted the *second* stage of advancement with this disturbing spirit of our land; and the impunity which it realized in its progress seemed to be a warrant for the still farther extension of its domain. And behold! the next step was an invasion of the political fabric of our country, by a crusade on the Southern States for the rescue of the slaves! By this time a mighty moral associated power had been arrayed for any violent enterprise that should be set on foot. The entire ranks had been well schooled in a thorough contempt of all opinions except their own, and seemed to think, that the whole world were under a moral obligation to respect and yield to theirs. Custom and law seemed to have no respect in their eyes *because* they were custom and law; but existing institutions were rather assumed to be wrong *because* they existed. They had found the religious world all wrong, and undertook to revolutionize it without scruple; they had found the conventional social state all wrong, and assumed the task of imposing new laws upon that; and now they have discovered that the political fabric of our country is wrong, and have begun to tear it down, without leave, and in open violation of the supreme law of the land. Before they had stepped foot upon this ground, they had nothing to oppose them, and success inspired confidence. Wrong themselves they could not be, in their own esteem; they have never dreamed of being wrong; it is not the nature of fanaticism. But this stepping out of the appropriate sphere of religious and moral reform, into the arena of political strife, under a vast and powerful political machinery of their own creation, puts them in a new position. The religious world, and the conventional social state, they might invade with impunity, and devastate at pleasure; there was no adequate power to withstand them; but a recognized and long established political fabric will not give way so easy.

Avaunt, ye infidels, and suspend your song of triumph, that religion is fallen, though it cannot be denied, that she is dishonored. She has been betrayed in her own house, and by her professed adherents: but their true character stands revealed. Christianity has never authorized such proceedings; but they are violations of her most sacred principles.

It requires but the slightest observation to justify the position we have assumed, as to the connexion between Abolitionism and other violent reforms. We do not, indeed, suppose it true, that all Abolitionists have been engaged in the other; or that all who may have taken part in the violences which came first, are engaged in the last. We only mean to aver, that there is not only a natural and common sympathy in all these movements, but that the most prominent leaders in any one of them, are generally found in all;

and that they are a flock which instinctively jump together over the same fence, when any one of them gives the lead. "We mean, moreover, to be understood as maintaining, that Abolitionism is only a new form of an old spirit, which, having found no great impediment in its former pranks, has thought fit to lay aside the comedy, and attempt the more grave enactment of a tragedy. This we regard as the philosophy of its history."

So far as Abolitionists themselves may turn their eyes upon these pages, we beg leave to assure them, that we mean nothing uncharitable by these remarks, or in our general treatment of this subject. They must be quite aware that the affluence of language has been exhausted, used up, and worn out, on their side, in epithets of censure on their opponents; and that they are the assailants in the most important particular. We believe, that the great majority of those, who have been drawn into the Abolition ranks, are honest, good people; but, that they are deceived. As we are convinced, that this business cannot go on much longer, in its present shape, without ruining the country, we therefore think the time has come, when the language of plainness is demanded, if, peradventure, the deluded may be undeceived; at least, that that portion of the public, not already committed to this cause, may clearly understand its character and position. It professes to be engaged in the cause of humanity and liberty; while in fact it leads directly to anarchy and bloodshed. It originated in violence, and has never lost its character—a violence which has been successively jumping from one line of movement, and from one object of assault, to another, acquiring strength in every stage of progress by the principle of organization. Finding, that its coercive measures did not answer all its purposes in the religious sphere, on account of certain obstacles existing in the state of public morals, it buckled on its armour for this new field, and applied the screw and lever to the dead weights found there. After working awhile with the same characteristic violence, and with some success, but on the whole, with a reasonable prospect of defeat, on account of its mode of operation, it jumped over into the political arena, where it now is, well at work with accumulated and accumulating powers; and what shall be the end thereof, heaven only knows; but it is, at least, a dangerous business. Of course, in consequence of the division of its forces, it can only carry on its former enterprises with diminished vigor, while it is supremely bent upon this. But the immense machinery that has been in operation, which is continually augmenting in its parts and power, is growing more and more formidable, and more and more efficient. Encountered it must be by the authorities of the nation, or else, in our opinion, it will soon force those authorities to resign their places.

CHAPTER VI
THE ABOLITION ORGANIZATION BORROWED FROM THE RELIGIOUS WORLD

We have nothing to do with the merits of the Religious and Benevolent Society system of this country; it is only necessary for us to allude to the character, skill, operation, and efficiency of its framework, to illustrate the fabric of the American Anti-Slavery Society, which has been constructed precisely after that model. To accomplish the various objects of the religious and benevolent public, they have thought it expedient and necessary to erect themselves, by association, into sundry bodies politic, or incorporations, which originally were small, but which have gradually grown to considerable importance. It has been found by experience, that by a skilful organization, and by an economical application of its means and agencies, a single Society, enjoying public favor, can operate upon the whole country, to secure interest, raise money, and carry on its designs. But the very necessities of the case have put in requisition a sort of State machinery, which, as is well known, has been erected, and in some instances extended, on a very large scale; and they are conducted with as much system, as the affairs of a Nation, not unfrequently with a superior tact and efficiency, as compared with the ordinary concerns of the political world. The fact, that rotation of office does not follow in these Societies, as in the State, gives them greater advantage in this particular. The various officers and agents become highly accomplished and skilled in their vocation, are supported by fixed and adequate salaries, and can devote themselves entirely to their work, from the day of their induction to the day of their death. They are at home in their several places and spheres, and know all about them. They understand by what means their objects can best be obtained, are always growing wiser by experience, and consequently more influential and powerful, in this particular. These Societies have always a Head; a Council Board; legislative, executive, and judicial departments of Government; Secretaries and Under-secretaries; a fiscal system; itinerating Agents; subsidiary organizations, multiplying in numbers, and increasing in influence; journals, periodicals, tracts, books, &c. &c.—all subserving their designs. These machineries are all the inventions of a single age, and constitute a new era in human

Society. They are, undeniably, institutions of great influence and power. For religious and benevolent objects, they seem to have been welcomed by the Christian world generally, have been encouragingly sustained; and some of them are engaged in large schemes, as wide as the human family, and might vie, in the extent of their correspondence and responsibilities, with the ordinary operations of political Governments. Confining themselves to the objects and cares which they have assumed before the public, they have neither roused the jealousies, nor encountered the opposition, of the political world. Their powers are of a high order, of great scope, and of no inconsiderable importance in the social system.

Exactly according to this pattern is the American Anti-slavery Society. The simple fact, that it has borrowed this machinery from this quarter, proves, that the argument of the previous chapter, showing it to be a religious movement, is founded in truth. Such, beyond all question, is its character. Neither is it any the less political on that account. The sum of the matter is: it is religion in the state; and so much *worse* than a *Union of Church and State*, as that it is a *usurpation*, set up in defiance of the State's authority, and in open violation of its highest, strongest, most sacred law!

It is well for the Churches of this land, that they are not engaged in this business, that they have lifted their voices against it, and acquitted themselves of its responsibilities. It would be enough to sink Christianity amongst us to the lowest depths, to rise again, no one could tell when. But, fortunately, the public, the world will see, that this responsibility rests on a few, and only a few, designing, ambitious, turbulent spirits; that the great majority of those who have been drawn into this mad enterprise, are perfectly innocent of any evil designs, have never dreamed of violating law, have had their best feelings worked upon by exaggerated statements and false representations, have been made to believe that this was their proper business, and been constituted Judges of that which did not belong to them, and which they know little or nothing about. We are disposed to believe, to hope, certainly, that it will only be necessary for them to be enlightened in the knowledge of their position, as members and abettors of such an organization, to be induced to withdraw, and wash their hands of its responsibilities. It is the moral power which their numbers give to it, that constitutes its importance and influence. It is in fact a vast and powerful machinery, from the very nature of its organization, and the methods of its operation, so long as it can hold its own; more especially, so long as it is in a state of actual growth, and in an advancing career. The Government of this country, and those States which are parties concerned, cannot be too much alive to this fact. The public generally ought to understand it; and if the knowledge and conviction should generally obtain, that this Society is a seditious organization, and engaged in a work of sedition, which, by continuance, may grow into treason, it is believed, that no more acquisitions to its numbers and power could be made, and that it would gradually die away, and cease to agitate the public mind, without the intervention of the public authorities.

We have shown, as we think, by the fairest argument, that this Society *is* an *organized* sedition. But even if there were any doubt upon the subject, that doubt ought to go in favour of public peace and safety—*Ne quid detrementi respublica capiat*—lest the republic receive damage.

If, in the judgment of the constituted authorities of this country, the public safety should require it, we have no more doubt of their competency to dissolve the American Anti-Slavery Society, and suppress its action as an organization, than of the power of a Court of Chancery to issue an injunction to arrest an alledged and apparent violation of law, till the case can be fairly tried. But whether, or when, it may be expedient, is for the proper authorities themselves, in their discretion, to decide. In such a case, the present component parts of this Society would be reduced to the Constitutional basis, with all the license of the Constitutional provisions; and on that ground they would be harmless. Whereas, as a *permanent* and *independent* political organization, they are an unconstitutional, vast, formidable, and dangerous power. This Society is in fact a rival Empire on the territories of the Republic; and the simple question is, whether this usurpation, or the old and Constitutional Government, shall stand. If this organization has *already* attained sufficient strength and confidence in its power, to refuse submission to the claims of the Constitution, and if it would *now* resist the empire of the law, in case it should be asserted, the very grave and portentious question arises, what is likely to be the state of things in this country, after the continued action and growth of this Society shall *compel* the Government to take a stand against it? There is all the difference between the two cases, as between the strength of a bud, and the vigorous trunk and extended arms of a full grown tree.

CHAPTER VII
THE ANARCHICAL PRINCIPLES
OF ABOLITIONISM

Nous verrons—Onward! seems to be alike the maxim and tendency of all violent reforms. It may be said, that Abolitionism has at last come to a fair and palpable *denoument*, in the formation of the *New England Non-resistence Society*, which was organized at Boston, in September, 1838, with William Lloyd Garrison, and such others, men and *women*, leaders. The fundamental principle of this new association is *identical* with that of the Abolition movement. Both hinge upon the same pivot. Indeed, it will be found, that all the violent reforms of our country are based upon this. It is stated in the Constitution of the Non-resistence Society in the following terms: "It appears to us a self-evident truth, that whatever the Gospel is designed to *destroy* at any period of the world, being contrary to it, ought *now* to be abandoned." The mischievous element of this proposition, as reduced to practice by the violent reformers, is *occult*, and would appear in its naked form by substituting for the last word "*abandoned*," that of *destroyed*—"ought *now* to be *destroyed*;" for these reformers do not admit, that those customs and laws, judged by their interpretation of the Gospel unlawful, may be retained till *persuasion* shall produce reform, and simply preach, that they "*ought* to be *abandoned*." But they clearly show their meaning is, that they "ought to be *destroyed*" and that it is not only lawful, but praiseworthy and a duty, to destroy them. *Destruction* is the ruling power of the code; and society, the world, is to take its chances for the setting up of a better state of things.

Now, we maintain, that this is a fair statement of the principles of Abolitionism, and of all other of the violent movements. Their doctrine of *immediatism*—if we may invent a new term—is always one and the same, and always has been. Wherever they find an evil, or wrong—*Down with it*—is the rule. *Fiat Justitia, ruat calum*—a sound principle, certainly; and a good maxim, in prudent hands; but a terrible one, in rash hands.

It is a good thing, and a very instructive result, that the principles of these Destructives have at last come out, and been openly published to the world, in the Constitution and "Bill of sentiments," adopted by the New England Non-resistance Society. There is now no longer a disguise. They openly renounce allegiance to all government: *"We cannot acknowledge allegiance to any human government!"* Here, then, it is, fairly ushered into the light of day—*a condition of universal anarchy*, the proclaimed Jubilee of these reformers. We have only to say, that this new Society has come honestly and openly to the end, to which all the *Immediatists* of whatever name, are rapidly advancing. The maxim—*Down with it*—which governs them all, and which is the soul, body, and foundation of their enterprise—cannot stop short of anarchy. There is nothing of importance in the avowed principles of this new Society, revolting and shocking as they are, which is not a legitimate consequence of Abolitionism; or, by the remotest degree of relationship, cousin-german to it. In the first place, they renounce allegiance to human government; the Abolitionists, to be consistent, ought to do the same; for they have made open war against it. *They* have announced the doctrine of *Immediatism* [1] as their fundamental principle; that also is the fundamental principle of the Abolitionists. *They* have levelled all distinctions in society, of rank, color, caste, and *sex*; and the doctrines of Abolitionism, carried out, have legitimately led them to this. *They* have proclaimed the Agrarian principle, in all forms of application, and denied the right of defending property, or any civil inheritance, by human authority, or force of arms; and Abolitionism requires the sanction of this principle to affect its designs. *They* recognise but one ruler—the King of heaven; it is equally necessary for the Abolitionists to set aside the authorities of earth. *They* have no country but the world, and no countrymen but mankind; the Abolitionists seem to be equally devoid of patriotism. *They* avow that neither nations, nor individuals, have a right to defend themselves against aggression; this will be convenient, and even necessary, to Abolitionists, in the execution of their plans. *They* pronounce the doctrine, that "the powers that be are ordained of God," "an absurd and impious dogma;" this, too, will be convenient to the Abolitionists, and it might be supposed, they had adopted it. *They* declare against all military preparations; we presume the Abolitionists are equally unfriendly to them, as they might prove uncomfortable opponents in their career. "As every human government is upheld by physical strength, and its laws enforced virtually at the point of the bayonet," *they* "repudiate all human politics" and legislation; the Abolitionists are equally averse to the "politics" and legislation of the slave-holding States, and of course to the political fabric of the Union. *They* deny the right of prosecution and indemnification for felony, which of course would be impossible, where there is no law; the Abolitionists deny the right of indemnification for the deprivation of property in slaves. *They* deny the right of all punishment for crimes; this would be extremely convenient for Abolitionists. *They* deny that their "doctrines are Jacobinical;" and why set up this defence before they are accused, except from the consciousness, that all the world will pronounce them so? The Abolitionists, too, as we think, are somewhat involved in this predicament. The members of this new Society are advocates of Non-resistance, *on one side*; and so are the Abolitionists: both are averse to being *opposed*, except so far as it may afford them the opportunity and title to plead the rights of the honest Connecticut negro's conscience, who, being asked by his master, what it said, replied, "Why, Massa, it says, I *won't*." But the members of this Society are to be great fighters, after all, and that, too, in the way of *aggression*, as they claim the right and declare the purpose of making war "boldly, by the application of their principles, upon all existing civil, political, legal, and ecclesiastical institutions;" that is, as one, remarking well on their scheme, hath it, "to take the greatest possible pains to get mobbed, persecuted, imprisoned, hung, and murdered." And little pity would they get. They, of course, are the framers of their own conscience, and its interpreters; and that is the empire, the rights of which they claim, under their professions of *Non-resistance*. Allow any man that, and what, repudiating the restraints of law, could he ask more?

> [1] The abstract notion, that whatever is judged to be wrong
> in the customs or laws of society, *may* and *must* be broken
> down, or rooted out, *forthwith*, without any regard to
> consequences.

But, notwithstanding the magisterial offices of society, they say, "We believe that the penal code of the old Covenant, '*An eye for an eye, and a tooth for a tooth*,' has been abrogated by Jesus Christ," &c. In other words, we suppose, they mean to set aside the authority of the Old Testament Scriptures; of course, the Decalogue: and *in* course, proceeding onward, the whole Bible. In this way, the Abolitionists would gain an important point, and procure the right of making a Bible to suit themselves. Thus endeth the career of violent reform — *in universal anarchy*. The New England Non-resistance Society is the climax; and it is remarkable, that there is scarcely a principle involved in the public declaration of their Creed, which, in some form of application, does not exactly suit the case and cause of the Abolitionists. — None, we apprehend, which does not very naturally and legitimately flow from it. *They were* Abolitionists in the previous stage of their career, and one of them was the founder of Abolitionism.[2] It only happens, that he still keeps the lead; and he and his present associates are only more consistent and more honest, in having opened the entire budget to the public gaze. There are, indeed, some few *outré* peculiarities of this new Association, ingeniously appended and incorporated, just enough to attract attention, and make it interesting as a curiosity. But there is nothing surprising in it, when we inquire into the causes which have generated the extravagant opinions, and set on foot the violent reforms, of our country. They may all be traced backward, through all their stages, and in all their connexions, under the broad and clear sun light of philosophical research.

> [2] Of Abolitionism in its modern garb of a violent reform—a totally, radically, and essentially, different thing from Emancipation in the sense attached to it before this agitation commenced. Abolitionism is now identified with an unconstitutional, and as we have proved, seditious interference of a combination of people in the free States, with the domestic condition of the slave States. It is shorn of the honors, both of a humane and patriotic enterprise, and merged in the responsibility of a political misdemeanor. This is the sense in which we use the term throughout this work; and we have supposed there was some foundation for ascribing the authorship of this movement to the gentleman above alluded to. Certainly, he was the most conspicuous actor, when it began to attract public attention. And behold! he is at the head, and we suppose at the bottom—(for we take for granted he must be the leader wherever he is)—of an Association set up professedly and without disguise, to overthrow all Government. This last stage—for we see not how it can go any further—is, in our esteem, an open and fair *denoument* of the principles of Abolitionism. Not, indeed, that the Abolitionists, as a body, have any such designs—for we charitably suppose, and fully believe, they have not— but the action of their fundamental principle of *immediatism*, to gain, by a *coup de main*, a visionary state of *perfectionism*, cannot stop short of this.

It is proper to remark, that, in the comprehensive picture given in this chapter, of the principles of the New England Non-resistance Society, we have taken the liberty to lay aside the garb in which they have presented them, except here and there a literal quotation, not only for brevity's sake, but to show them in their naked form. We think, however, that we have not misrepresented; and even if we have done so, in any slight shades, the moiety of this delicious *morceau*, is enough to show the *taste* of those who have swallowed it, and how the *physic* is likely to operate. As to the feature of *non-resistance*, it is what is vulgarly called a "fudge," they having reserved to themselves the privilege of conscience, according to their own interpretation of its prerogatives, and moreover declared their resolute and unflinching purpose to *"assail* all existing institutions." Besides, this *pretension*, to adopt their own language, is "a measure of sound policy;" for they could not otherwise be tolerated for a moment; and they hope to gain sympathy by *appearing* not to resist, while they themselves are engaged in *open war* on every thing that is valuable and dear to society. To show the connexion between this and things that had gone before, it is only necessary to quote one sentence from their own hand: "The triumphant progress of the cause of *Temperance* and *Abolition* in our land ... *encourages us* to *combine* our own means and efforts for the promotion of a still greater cause." Far be it from us, however, by this allusion, to disparage the Temperance reformation, any farther than the violent and overstrained part of it is concerned. And this qualification, we trust, will be satisfactory to all, whose good opinion we have any hope of enjoying.

CHAPTER VIII
THE INCENDIARY DOCTRINES
OF ABOLITIONISM

Facit per alium, facit per se. The accessory to a crime is by law, and in justice, made responsible with the principal. No man can deny, that the effect of the Abolition doctrines and measures on the slave-holding States, if they were not resisted, would speedily lead to insurrection and massacre; that scenes of this horrible kind would be constantly occurring, till the whole South would become a field of desolation. It is true, the Abolitionists say, it would not be so, if the slave-holders would give up. This, however is a justification, which, we suppose, is not likely to be admitted. Everybody knows, that the slave-holders will not give up, and that they are more remote from it now than when this agitation commenced. The Abolitionists are responsible for having, by their imprudence and rashness, rivetted the chains of slavery, and put far off the day of Emancipation, unless they shall succeed in breaking up society, by forcing abolition—the responsibility of which, we apprehend, would be immeasureably greater than that which now rests upon them. The right or wrong of slavery cannot now be discussed with any effect, because another great question has forced that aside. It is the question, whether the political fabric of the country, in relation to this subject, shall give way to violence? The claim of the slave to his freedom, we think, will never be listened to, till that is settled. We must take things as they are, and man as he is.

"No," says the Abolitionist, "God forbid. We stick to *principle*; and our principle is, that the slave has a right to his freedom—a right paramount to any artificial and accidental state of society that exists, standing in the way of it; and the consequences of opposing this claim, *be* on those who take this stand." Is this a fair statement? We are inclined to think it is, as to those Abolitionists who lead and govern the cause. Certainly, we should be willing to state it in any other form, if we could do it more fairly. We only wish to know on what ground they stand, that we may know how to take them. From all we have been able to learn of their principles, we believe that the above statement does them no injustice.

Let us, then, observe the following facts: The slave-holders are resolved they will not give up; the Abolitionists are resolved they shall. The more the latter do, in the way they are now engaged, to accomplish their end, so much the more determined are the former to maintain what they claim to be their rights. The former point, first, to the Federal Constitution, as their security; next, to their own swords. Such, undoubtedly, is the true state of the case. The right of the slave to his freedom, as claimed by the Abolitionists in his behalf, is out of the question, till this political warfare is ended; and every step makes the case worse and worse. Such is the present position of the cause of Abolition in this country: the Abolitionists stick to their principle, that "the duty, safety, and best interests of all concerned, require the *immediate abandonment*" of slavery. Such is the language of their Constitution, italicised as above; and they are accustomed to press that principle by all the means in their power, *without regard to consequences*; and we think it may be fairly added, as a general fact, *without respect to the supreme law of the land*, which happens to be against them. They view the right claimed for the slave *paramount to all law that stands opposed*. We believe we do not mistake in this. Every one may see what such principles, carried out and enforced, lead to; and when we consider the certainty of their being opposed, and opposed to the last, we think it not unjust to pronounce them *incendiary* in their character.

We will illustrate this state of things by a case of fact. We happened to be acquainted with a very estimable and exemplary clergyman, some ten years ago, or more, mild and benevolent in his disposition, bland in his manners, of unquestionable piety, and in all respects agreeable; but we observed, with some concern, that he appeared to be tending strongly to the way of violent reforms. In the spring of 1838 we were glad to meet him again, as an old friend; but found him thoroughly in for Abolition, according to the modern type. In the course of conversation, it was suggested, that Abolition, hardly pushed, would chance to make some bad work. "No matter," said the gentleman, "the principle is sacred." "And must be maintained at all events?" "Certainly." "But it may occasion the effusion of blood." "We can't help it." "There will be insurrections and massacres." "That is the fault of those who committed the first sin; and they must take the consequences." It will be seen, that they who committed the first sin, were out of the way many generations ago, and were never citizens of this country. "But, do you mean to advocate the *instant* manumission of all slaves, without regard to consequences?" "Certainly. Slavery is sin; and all sin ought to be left off instantly." "But do you not see, that slavery is interwoven with a complicated state of society, political and domestic; and that it is impossible to do it away *immediately*?" "No matter; it is wrong, and ought not to continue a moment." "But your doctrine will produce anarchy." "No—God will take care of that. God never required any thing, that will produce a bad result. Obedience to his will is always safe; and disobedience unsafe. Slavery is sin; and all sin should be repented *now*, radically and thoroughly, in practice as well as in heart." "But, there is the law of the land." "And there is the law of God, and of nature." "But the law of God says, *the powers that be are ordained of God. Put them in mind to be subject to principalities and powers, and to obey magistrates.*" "That is a general rule, and was never intended to vitiate the authority of conscience. If it is to be construed strictly, and without exception, we had never had the Protestant Reformation, nor American Independence. The indefeasible rights of conscience, and of liberty, in the sense now maintained, may always be asserted, and ought to be." "But may we go on a crusade, in behalf of others, for these objects?" "Thou shalt love thy neighbour as thyself, and shalt not suffer sin upon thy brother." "Then you are in favor of carrying Abolition *forthwith*, as best it can be done, in despite of the law of the land, and without regard to consequences?" "Undoubtedly. It is impossible, there should be a higher law, than that asserted in this cause. The law of the land will never be altered, if we let it alone; and the only way to bring it about, is to press matters by agitation. There are always enough on the side of order, and we have no fear of consequences in so good and holy an enterprise," &c. &c.

We have abridged this dialogue, and profess no more than to give the substance of it. And when we compare it with all we have seen, heard, and read on the side of Abolition, and with the ordinary features of the movement, we see not but it is a fair representation. Any persons, however, are at liberty to qualify it, as they may think it deserves. There are, doubtless, Abolitionists of all shades and degrees; but there is a common ground, on which those who constitute the strength of the movement, meet. We suppose it ought to be allowed, that most of them *profess* respect for the authority of law on this point, and that they intend nothing but Constitutional modes of reformation. The Constitution of their great Society, proposes "to do all that is *lawfully* in our power to bring about the extinction of slavery." But every one construes the law for himself; and generally, that is lawful, which sets up the right of the slave to his freedom, as paramount to the law of the land. That we do no injustice to Abolitionists by these statements, is open to proof, by the high authority of the last Annual Report of their

Parent Society, in which, however startling it may seem, they have not only in effect, *but in form*, set aside the authority of the Federal Constitution, in regard to slavery, by *construction*! After quoting the well known third clause of the second Section of the Fourth Article, which recognizes the validity of property in slaves, and provides to defend it, having first stated, that, "if strictly construed it could not apply to slaves," because it does not *name* them *as slaves*, the Report goes on to say: "It is obvious to remark, in the first place, that the *intentions* of the framers—*whatever by historical evidence we may ascertain them to have been*—*cannot bind* us to an interpretation of the Constitution which its own language does not render necessary, and which is inconsistent with objects for which it was professedly framed, to wit, 'to establish justice,' and 'to secure the blessings of liberty.' *But we go further*: We contend, that when the Constitution was framed, it was the understanding of *all parties*, that slavery was soon to be abolished by the States, and the clause intended to facilitate the recovery of fugitive slaves was a mere *temporary* concession, to *expire* with the unhallowed anomaly which called for it. If such be the case, it need hardly be said, that the slave States, after having *violated*, on their part, that good faith which was implied in the compact, *have no right* to urge its fulfilment, beyond the letter, on the other part." "Beyond the letter." "The *letter*" does not happen to *name* slaves.

Now, if *this* is not *coming out*, and by the highest authority, by their own solemn and sanctioned Annual Scripture, declaring *null* and *void* the law of the land, and its highest law, in relation to the subject of controversy, it might be difficult to say what would be so. They even set aside the universally established rule of interpretation, confessing to the *intention* of the law, but denying its authority. Henceforth the public may know what to expect. We think, that, with this document lying before our eyes, it is no libel to say, the Abolitionists *do not respect the law*; and that they have made up their minds, to trample it under foot. Their measures, and their language, would certainly imply it. They seem to be so far carried away by their sympathy for the slaves, that the hazard of causing to flow in rivers the best blood of the land, by a civil war, seems hardly sufficient to effect an abatement of their zeal; and if the slave-holders and their families, should be butchered in the strife of Abolition, "that is the fault of those who committed the first sin, and they must take the consequences." *Immediate, instant emancipation* is the word and the *principle, whatever comes*. There is no law above it—none that must not give way to it. Let the public judge, whether this principle be not incendiary, and sanguinary, in the most revolting aspects. The only barrier, hitherto supposed to stand in its way, the Federal Constitution, is swept away by an authoritative commentary, and the license to go forth to battle, has, by this act, received the sanction of the Supreme Legislative Assembly and high Court of the American Anti-Slavery Society!

We think the time has come, when the public of this country have a right to demand, whether the Abolitionists do indeed intend thus to *force* the application of their principles, in contempt of law, and at the hazard of all consequences. Let them avow this scheme openly, and it will be enough. The uncharitable imputation of occult criminal designs is unwarrantable. But we submit, whether the passage just quoted from the Annual Report of this Society is not sufficiently open; and whether the habitual developements of the great movement, as made before the public, in so many forms, do not corroborate and confirm the impression which this document is calculated to produce?

CHAPTER IX
POLITICAL RESPONSIBILITY IN REGARD TO SLAVERY

We believe the Abolitionists are accustomed to find one apology for the movement in which they are engaged, in the assumption, that all the Members of the American Union are responsible for the existence of slavery therein, if not equally, yet in part; and being conscientiously opposed to slavery, their conscience obliges them to act in obedience to its dictates. They cannot, therefore, choose to abstain from this enterprise, if they would. We propose here to consider this question, as it cannot be denied, if the assumption be founded in truth and justice, that there is some weight in the statement. It is obviously proper to begin at the *beginning*, and enquire where the responsibility rests for introducing slavery into this country.

We say, therefore, that it was imposed upon this country against the avowed wishes, and resolute remonstrances of the ancestors of those, who now have charge of the evil that was thus entailed; and that resistance to the imposition came to the brink of a rebellion—nay, was a cause of rebellion.

"So early as 1502, the Spaniards begun to employ a few negroes in the mines of Hispaniola; and in the year 1517, the Emperor, Charles V., granted a patent to certain persons for the exclusive supply of 4000 negroes annually, to the islands of Hispaniola, Jamaica, Cuba, and Puerto Rico."[3] John Hawkins, an Englishman, received the honors of knighthood, and was made Treasurer of the Navy, by Queen Elizabeth, for his achievements in the slave trade. Elizabeth, James I., Charles I., and II., were all in the habit of chartering companies to carry it on. Charles II., his brother, the Duke of York, noblemen, gentry, and *ladies* of high rank and quality, were subscribers to these companies; and England, Europe, revolted not at the deed! The public conscience of the world seemed to tolerate it! When the slave trade first commenced, from Great Britain, under Elizabeth, the American Colonies did not exist. The succeeding princes patronized the traffic, and introduced slavery into their American provinces. "In 1760, South Carolina, a British Colony, passed an act to prohibit further importation; but Great Britain rejected this act with indignation, and declared that the slave trade was beneficial and necessary to the mother country. The Governors of the Colonies had *positive orders* to sanction no law enacted against the slave trade. In Jamaica, in the year 1765, an attempt was made to abolish the trade to that island. The Governor declared, that his instructions would never allow him to sign the Bill. It was tried again in 1774, but Great Britain, by the Earl of Dartmouth, President of the Board, answered: *We cannot allow the Colonies to check or discourage, in any degree, a traffic so beneficial to the nations.*"[4]

[3] Bryant Edward's West Indies.

[4] Professor Dew's Review of the Debate in the Virginia legislature, of 1831-'32.

The history of legislation, in the Colony of Virginia, records *twenty-three* Acts, imposing duties on the importation of slaves, with the avowed design of suppressing the trade. "In 1772, most of the duties, previously imposed, were re-enacted, and the Assembly transmitted, at the same time, a petition to the Throne, of which the following are extracts:—

"'We are encouraged to look up to the Throne, and *implore* your Majesty's paternal assistance, in averting a calamity of a most alarming nature.... The importation of slaves into the Colonies from the coast of Africa, hath long been considered a trade of *great inhumanity*, and under its present encouragement, we have too much reason to fear, will endanger the very existence of your Majesty's American dominions. Deeply impressed with these sentiments, we most *humbly beseech* your Majesty *to remove all those restraints* on your Majesty's Governors of this Colony, which prohibit such laws as might check so very pernicious a commerce.'

"The *first* Assembly which met in Virginia, after the adoption of her Constitution, prohibited the traffic; and '*the inhuman use of the royal prerogative*' against the action of the Colony upon this subject, is enumerated in the *first* clause of the first Virginia Constitution, *as a reason of the separation from the mother country.*"[5]

[5] Professor Dew.

Such was the *common* feeling of the Southern Colonies, though more decidedly manifested in Virginia. They never invited, they never tempted the slave trade, except by a silent acquiescence for a season, in what was imposed upon them by the cupidity of foreigners, and the mandates of authority, before the public conscience of mankind had begun to remonstrate; and the moment they opened their eyes to its domestic results among themselves, they set their faces, and employed all their lawful powers, against it.

"Federal America interdicted the slave trade from her ports *thirteen* years before Great Britain; she made it punishable as a crime *seven* years before, she fixed *four* years sooner the period of non-importation—which period was earlier than that determined upon by Great Britain for her Colonies."[6]

[6] Walsh's Appeal.

For the introduction of Slavery into America, therefore, the Americans themselves are acquit of all political responsibility. All that can be said is, that individuals purchased slaves that were brought and offered, when the public conscience of the world tolerated the traffic; but it was under the authority, and by the imposition, of a parent Government, in another Continent, that slavery was reared into a domestic and political institution, the process all the while having been solemnly protested against by those whose voice had a claim to be heard, and who were most intimately concerned, until it grew into a magnitude and importance, too formidable to be dealt with by a violent hand of excision and extirpation—sufficiently formidable, indeed, to demand the utmost wisdom and prudence of man for its treatment and ultimate disposal.

Thus, having fairly wiped from the American escutcheon the political responsibility of introducing slavery in this Continent, and among ourselves, it remains to be considered, how far the present generation of slaveholding Americans are responsible for this state of things. The sum of the matter lies in one short sentence: *They were born into the world the heirs of this condition.* In no manner or degree are they responsible for it, any farther than they maintain it, and *as* they maintain it. We suppose the Abolitionists themselves would not differ widely from us here, except as, peradventure, some of them may take their stand on the theological proposition—"In Adam's fall we sinned all." If, however, it may be assumed, that all agree on this point, it is the simple and the great question at issue. The slave States say, that is *their* business; and the Abolitionists say, it is *ours.* This is the *contest*—the question *to be tried.*

And one of the apologies of the Abolitionists, for interference in this concern, is, that the whole nation is involved in the responsibility. Let us see, whether this be true. It must be admitted, that it requires some study to comprehend the nature of our political fabric, as a nation, with the relations of its parts to each other, and to the Unity; but still, like a mathematical problem, though obscure and misty to the intellect, before it is laid down and demonstrated step by step, it is afterwards no less clear and satisfactory. It happens, that this task has already been done in a former chapter, and requires only to be restated here. The great principle, and its whole scope, are laid down before the eye, in the tenth Article of the Federal Constitution. By this rule, the respective States are declared possessed, by original right, of all independent and sovereign powers, not "delegated or prohibited" by the Federal Constitution. In these limited attributes of sovereignty, therefore, they are placed precisely on the footing of all other independent States and Nations; and as the institution of slavery, and all legislation over it, is one of these "reserved" powers, it follows, that all its responsibility devolves on those States, in which it exists, and is maintained. It is impossible it should extend any farther, from the nature of the compact. It is a simple proposition, and may be understood by any body, by a child, that I cannot be responsible for that which the laws of society forbid me to meddle with; and this is precisely the proposition which sets forth and limits the responsibility of slavery in the United States. The Union was formed on these conditions, and in an exigency under which the parties were forced to combine for common good, with mutual concessions thus specified, in the same manner as a society of any individual persons is formed by mutual compact and mutual concession, and the responsibility of every member is limited by the line thus marked out. As he is not permitted to trespass on the rights secured to others, he cannot be held responsible for any thing that would demand such a trespass. If the rights thus secured are invaded, or violated, the administration of justice does not devolve on individual members of the community, or on any combination not provided for by law, but on the constituted and public authorities. Even though there be manifest injustice for which the law does not provide a remedy, or injustice sanctioned by law, the same principle applies, and the evil can be redressed only by a constitutional legislation.

But, it is said, the principle of slavery is incorporated and sanctioned in the Federal Constitution; and we are all at least so far responsible. This, surely, will not be urged by Abolitionists, who have formally and publicly declared, by their own mode of legislation, as shown in the previous chapter, that this principle has ceased to exist, and is no longer binding. But suppose it does exist. It neither declares, nor sanctions, the *right* of slavery *as such*: but simply interposes the authority of a principle, which applies equally to all the States, to enable them to maintain and secure their domestic institutions, as established by their sovereign will—a principle, which may accidentally operate more in favour of one State, than of another, but which is equally important to all, and is habitually employed by all. The Government of the United States, therefore, is not responsible in this matter, politically considered; and therefore not responsible at all, as it exists only as a political institution. All these public relations are political, and can involve no other responsibility than that which is prescribed by the laws of the social state, as it exists. The relation of the master to the slave involves a responsibility which applies to private conscience, and the master must answer for it. So also the relation of the master to that political commonwealth which maintains slavery; and he must answer for that, to the extent of his political influence and relations. And so with every member of such a commonwealth; but farther than this, he cannot be held to account. This, we think, is the legitimate domain of conscience, and the limit of responsibility, in regard to this subject.

But, it will yet be said, that the Government of the United States is the public guardian of slavery, by the force and habitual application of the fourth article of the Federal Constitution; and therefore, all the citizens of the Republic are involved in this responsibility, and consequently have a right to concern themselves about it. Notwithstanding, it cannot be denied, that the Federal compact bars this claim; and the Christian's conscience might find its salvo in the Scripture which saith—"He shall abide in the Tabernacle and holy hill of the Lord, who sweareth to his own hurt, and changeth not." In the day of trial, our fathers swore to this compact, and bound their children in the covenant, if we accept the inheritance; if not, then we have no voice in the matter. But, we think, the political pledge of the general Government to maintain the domestic institutions of the several States, in case of need, so far as they do not interfere with the prerogatives "delegated," or those "prohibited," does not involve a responsibility for the *character* of those institutions—not at all.

The *Union* is admitted to have been indispensible to our National Independence, and the slave States came into it on the condition, that the institution of slavery should not be disturbed, and that it should be maintained in the way the Federal Constitution prescribes. Whether slavery was right or wrong in itself, or how long it should be maintained, were questions never submitted; but were left among the "reserved" rights. The Union never had any responsibility in the existence of slavery; it never assumed any; it has never had any whatever; it has only covenanted to protect the sovereign rights of the slave States, as it has the sovereign rights of all other States, leaving to them the sovereign control over their own domestic institutions, without assuming any one item of responsibility in regard to their character. The principle which forbids the interference of the Union, absolves it from responsibility.

But still the Abolitionist holds his ground, as a religionist, and declares, that he is bound to have a care for all his fellow creatures, and to help them, wherever he sees them laboring under any evils, physical or moral, or any wrongs social or political. So far as his benevolence extends to those who suffer under social and political wrongs, if they happen to be beyond the limits of his own Commonwealth, we can only give him a piece of advice, which he may use or not, at his own discretion, viz. that, till the world gets to be in a more favorable state for the range of his sympathies, as a religionist claiming to carry his religion into politics by force, he had better be content with the wisdom of Moses, who, as it would seem, saw fit, not only to tolerate, but to *legalize*, slavery—for whatever may be said of *different forms*, it cannot be denied that the *principle* was there. Or, with the wisdom of the Apostle Paul, who, instead of interfering with the political fabrics of his time, in regard to this as well as other matters, sent back Onesimus, a runaway slave, thereby recognizing the legal claim of his master, Philemon, with such messages as these: "If he hath wronged thee, or oweth thee ought, put that to my account.... Whom I would have *retained* ... but *without thy mind* would I do nothing.... Though I might be much bold in Christ to *enjoin* thee that which is convenient, yet for love's sake I rather *beseech* thee." Or, with the wisdom of the Apostle Peter, who said: "Servants, be subject to your Masters with all fear—not only to the *good* and *gentle*, but to the *froward*. And what glory is it, if, when ye shall be buffetted for your faults, ye take it patiently; but if, when ye do well, and suffer for it, ye take it patiently, this is acceptable to God." It is also written by "such an one as Paul, the aged: Let as many servants as are *under the yoke*, count their own Masters worthy of all honor, that the name of God and his doctrines be not blasphemed, &c. *These things*," saith he to Timothy, "*teach* and *exhort*." For, we think, the Abolitionist would be much better employed in imitating these illustrious examples, than by inculcating sedition, and stirring up insurrection. Or, if this should not suit his taste, then we would advise him by all means, to let the politics of foreign States alone, as it is a delicate and dangerous business, not as yet tolerated by the actual state of society. If he thinks so, he may rely upon it, he has made a mistake.

If, however, he insists on being thus occupied, and since his labors are not well received in the slave holding States of America, and seem likely to do more hurt than good, we would advise him to "shake off the dust off his feet against them," and turn to another field, and still *more* remote, as he likes distant objects. If he would do the greatest amount of good, and since he is resolved to have a *foreign* field, let him try where the evil exists in more aggravated forms. For there is actually less slavery in the United States, in proportion to the population, and the whole of it in a milder form, than in any other part of the world, civilized or uncivilized. For what is the *name* of a thing, apart from its essential attributes? Slavery, fairly defined, is the unequal and unjust depression of man in relation to his fellow man, as the result of an artificial state of society, which has been erected, and is maintained for the advantage of the few, and to the disadvantage of the many. The degree of depression, and the amount of *oppression*, are accidental. Both are greater in any other part of the world that can be named, beyond the bounds of the United States, than in the slave States of the South—if, perhaps, we except the North American British Provinces—now being invaded on Abolition principles.

If the Abolitionists are resolved to interfere with the domestic condition of other States for the relief of the oppressed, and cannot otherwise satisfy their consciences, let them go to England, to Ireland, and to the British manufactories. We assure them, they will find work enough there, and enough of slavery too, as that particular form of evil is especially to their taste. Let them go to the Continent of Europe, and they will find enough of it any where in that field—more especially in Italy, in Spain and Portugal, in Hungary, in Poland, and above all, in Russia. Let them go to the tribes and nations that border on the shores of the Mediterranean; let them penetrate into Northern, Southern, and Eastern Asia; it is all a ripe field for their sickle, or if they like it better, for their sword—for it will no doubt soon come to that. Let them go to Africa—which their sympathies would naturally lead them to first—and there, independent of the temptations and effects of the slave traffic, as all travellers inform us, they will find slavery in such amount, and in forms of such horrid and murderous cruelty, as to show the fields of its abode in the Southern States a paradise in comparison. There they will see, that it is better to be a slave in America, than a free man in Africa, without justifying slavery; and that the best conditions of African barbarism could never be envied by the worst of American slavery, if both were equally well known to the parties, having their option between the two. There they might learn, that God, in his high and inscrutable providence, can bring good out of evil, and that, by the lights of American civilization, and the blessings of American Christianity, thrown out upon Africa from these shores, that long suffering, abused, and "pealed" race, may yet hope to receive some indemnification for their bleeding wrongs.

But do the Abolitionists reply, "that if we enter on the fields of Europe, or of any other countries, for political action, by any efficient force, to rescue the oppressed, we shall lose our heads." That, indeed, may be a wise thought. Or, "if we attempt it by secret operations, and by emissions of the press, clandestinely introduced, we shall embroil our country in a foreign war." There is little doubt of that. Or, "if we organize a political machinery at home, industriously occupying years of preparation for descent, waiting for an opportunity, and it is known that our force is likely to tell with effect, when the time of aggressive action shall arrive, it will produce the same result, unless our own Government shall interpose, and suppress our movement." This, too, is doubtless a fair conclusion. But, let it be remembered, that a foreign war is infinitely less to be dreaded, than a domestic and civil one; and that it is no less certain, if the Abolition movement is not suppressed, we must have the last. The cases are parallel: as a foreign Nation could not endure such interference, neither can the slave States of the South. There is as valid and justifiable a right of interference in one case, as in the other, and an equal provocation for resort to arms, if the General Government should not interpose its authority, and arrest the movement.

CHAPTER X
THE ROMANCE OF ABOLITIONISM

We live in an age of romantic sympathy and religious sentimentalism. There is a charity that prefers a remote object, to one that is near. A blind beggar, with every appearance of want and wretchedness, sits daily by the way side, to ask alms. Floods of population swim along, and now and then he gets a penny; but no body stops to ask him of his misery, or sympathize with his woes. He is a solitary, uncheered being during the day, in the midst of a busy, moving, and apparently happy world; and as night comes on, he feels his way to his wretched hovel, if he has one, and lies down in rags and filth, to sleep as he can. He may, or may not, have some one to comfort him there; but the world never asks. In every crowded population there are hundreds of poor and wretched beings, whose wants are fruitful of sorrow, and whose pains are without relief. They live in misery, and die without comfort; and that, too, while surrounded with an affluence that knows not how to dissipate its treasures. The sound of the light steps of the happy is heard in the street, but they enter not the uninviting abode to inquire into the wants of its tenants; the carriages of the wealthy roll onward; but the suffering poor, so near at hand, are not remembered. Even if you apply to the public in their behalf, you will chance to receive for answer, "they are worthy of their doom, and are only reaping the wages of their sins. We have known them well, and generally speaking, there is little merit, and a slender reward, in relieving such objects."

But, form a Society of these very persons, and send out an Agent to the Antipodes to hunt up the misery that may be found there, to report in due form on precisely the same cases of distress, or on such, perhaps, as are not half so worthy of pity, and the tear of sympathy will be seen trickling down the cheek of the sentimentalist, as he reads the printed document in his easy chair, or listens to the fervid eloquence of the platform orator, who feels the same pleasure in telling the story which his hearers do in receiving it. "'Tis distance lends enchantment," and because these persons can luxuriate in the indulgence of their benevolence in agreeable circumstances, without being compelled to come in actual contact with the squalid and disgusting forms of misery; or like Howard, to sacrifice home and comfort to look it up, and administer consolation at the expense of ease and better society.

To all this we have no objection. Even if the statements are exaggerated, and the pictures highly colored; though the Agents engaged in this work know well, that their support depends on the interest they create; though there is not half the good accomplished that was dreamt of, or is supposed; nay, though all the fruits of this sympathy were expended on the way to its objects, and in sustaining this machinery, still the world is made better, and the compensation is abundant, though nothing else be gained, but the good and kind feeling it has kindled up at home. It is even better, that they who will not relieve the miserable objects that lie at their doors, or perish in the streets, or starve in the comfortless abodes of their own city or town, should have some small pittances of their abundance drawn out by the workings of a romantic sympathy for the remotest objects, than that they should do nothing at all. If they feel not for the wretched before their eyes, it is yet good that they can be made to feel for those who are far off.

The Christian missions of the age, and all purely benevolent enterprises, which meddle not with the political structures of society, are most worthy of patronage and support, *under a suitable organization*. However they may, in some degree, fall under these strictures, our remarks are only an echo of practical and faithful missionaries, who have themselves written largely on the romance of Missions, and laboured to chasten the views and expectations of contributors to the cause, and to establish the work on the basis of sound Christian principle. As we have before intimated, the Abolition movement is a wandering star, an eccentric and fiery orb, that has broken loose from the Religious and Benevolent Society system, with all its armor on, and betrayed and violated the principles of that system, by plunging into the battle field of political strife, and running riot in a wild and mad encounter with the political interests of mankind. It is a comet out of place, thrown off from its own sphere by the violence of its centrifugal action, and comes dashing on its way into a family of planetary worlds, whose orderly course around a common centre it threatens to throw into confusion, and is likely to plunge full sweep on that great central orb which gives us light and heat, and which, we hope and pray, will be able to sustain the shock without injury.

The romance of Abolitionism is well illustrated in the history of that crusade which roused all Europe, and led forth its armies upon the plains of Western Asia against the infidels, to rescue "the Holy City" from "the abomination of desolation;" and we will venture to say, that the great majority of Abolitionists are equally and no more wise, in the expedition to which they are lending their aid. They know just as much of the real state of things in the slave-holding States, and seem to be equally blind to the romantic character of the enterprise.

Let it be always understood, that we make no controversy with the Abolitionists, as to the right or wrong of slavery, in this country or any other, or in any case whatever. For in all cases, we presume, that we are as much opposed to slavery as they are. We consider, that this question is entirely forced aside by the position assumed by the Abolitionists, and by principles they have avowed before the public, which must necessarily supercede this question, till those principles are practically settled. Abolitionists claim the right to a political interference, which is denied to them alike by the Constitutional law of the land, by the expressed opinions of our national authorities, by the parties most intimately concerned, and by the general voice of public opinion. And this is the ground upon which we meet them, and only upon this ground. We have no objection to their opinion concerning the inexpediency and sin of slavery, or to any proper modes of expressing that opinion. This has long been known to be the common opinion of the North, without disturbing society in the South; and the action of that opinion, in a proper way, was likely to make advances, and ultimately to gain its object, if it had not been checked by this inauspicious interference with existing political society and political claims. Abolition, in the peculiar circumstances and relations of American political society, can never, as we think, be *enforced* by political action from abroad; it can only be gained through the moral sense of those who have the charge of slavery, in connexion with their interests. While, therefore, we declare the general ignorance of Abolitionists of the real state of slavery, as a reason why they should not meddle with it in the way they propose, we protest against being represented as the apologist of slavery.

Since, therefore, the people of the North cannot interfere *politically* with the slavery of the South—for we deem ourselves entitled to assume this ground, in view of the reasons already presented—and since a wide spread and powerful political combination is in the field, mustering additional forces, and stirring up their ranks to an onward course, by exaggerated and unfair representations, we think it important, by all suitable means, to endeavour to break that spell of romance, which, we conceive, has no small share in this undertaking. We say, then, that the great body of Abolitionists have not the means of knowing, and consequently do not know, the real condition of slavery in the States where it exists, either as to what it is in itself, or as to what it is in comparison of other states of society in this and other countries. Instructed and excited by the documents and various literary emissions of the Society—all of which appear to be greatly exaggerated in their representation of facts, inflammatory in their character, and some of the most influential of them purely fictitious—they have obtained views of slavery at the South which cannot be sustained by the truth of the case, and have been stirred up to a sympathy which is for the most part romantic. *All* their views of the practicability of that form of action they have assumed, being itself an unlawful organisation, as we have shown, and at war with the political structure of our society, are, as we think, purely romantic. They are generally, therefore, involved in an atmosphere of romance on this subject.

As to the practicability of *immediate emancipation*—which is the avowed doctrine and aim of the Abolitionists—either for the good of the slaves, or the safety of society, it receives the unqualified negative of all Northern men and foreigners, who have visited the slave-holding States, without having been previously committed to the principles of Abolitionism; and that, too, against all the reports that have been brought from the British West Indies, down to this time, by the Agents of the American Anti-Slavery Society, or through other more circuitous or direct channels. Every practical man may see, that the experiment of emancipation in the West Indies is not yet fairly tested. We have read Thome's & Kimball's "Six Months' Tour" and Professor Hovey's "Letters," and compared them with other evidence and the unalterable principles of human nature; and after making those abatements which experience teaches are always due to ex parte statements, we honestly conceive, that the argument is neutralised, and the whole subject is necessarily left in suspense as to the legitimate influence of such testimony.

We say, then, without fear of contradiction, that every disinterested *man's* report from the South, whether American or foreigner, on the question of *immediate abolition*, declares decidedly and solemnly to the Abolitionists, "Gentlemen, you are wrong. It is impossible."

But the doctrine of *immediate* abolition, *dictated* to the slave-holding States, and *imposed* upon them, even though it were safely practicable, assumes the right of interference, and therefore cannot be expected to be conceded by those concerned, and who claim the right of originating and deciding this question for themselves. The same right has been claimed by the Northern States, where slavery formerly existed, and in no case have they seen fit to attempt *immediate* emancipation. To enforce it upon the South by foreign dictation would be despotic, nay, an invasion, and, as we think, "contrary to the principles of our republican form of Government." We declare, in the first place, that foreign, that is, Northern Abolitionists are, from the necessities of their position, *incompetent* judges of this question; and next, that they are unconstitutional, and therefore unlawful judges. Certainly, we do not mean by this to debar the right of opinion, or any constitutional modes of expressing it; but only, that they have no right to sit in judgment on this question for the purposes of dictation and legislation, or for that which is tantamount to legislation, to *enforce* this principle.

Moreover, some of the most influential literary emissions of the American Anti-Slavery Society are *purely fictitious*, and generally so exaggerated and highly coloured, or so unfaithful in not giving the whole truth, as to misrepresent the truth. "The narrative of James Williams," which has probably had more influence, and excited more feeling, than any other single document, and which was thought of sufficient importance to be made conspicuous in the last Annual Report of the Society, by devoting one third of a page *to attest its veracity*, notwithstanding the Abolitionists had been sufficiently advised, *that it was false*. They have at last been forced to make public confession, *that it is a fiction*! It is impossible to say, what proportion of the issues of this Society are of this character, because the proof of a negative, especially in such matters, is always slow and difficult; but the exceeding avidity of the Abolitionists to take up and accredit such stories as "the Narrative of James Williams," directly in the face of rebutting and conclusive evidence, and the strong temptations in such circumstances to fiction, may fairly establish the presumption, that many of their issues are purely fictitious.

But exaggeration of statement, over-coloring of facts, and keeping back parts of truth which are essential to a correct judgment, are precisely of the nature of fiction. Such is the concurrent testimony from all quarters, and such the evidence of probability in the very nature of things, that this part of the budget must be immense. Every body, who has visited the slave States, *knows*, that slavery there is *not* what it is represented to be in the publications of the American Anti-slavery Society, in general, or in particular. Certain specific evils, necessarily resulting from a system of slavery, no fair man can deny; that some of these are of a revolting character, candor requires to be confessed; that there are cruel and inhuman masters, is no less true. So also are there cruel and inhuman parents, husbands, masters of indented apprentices, and various other superiors in the relations of life, *out* of the slave States. We will venture to say, from authoritative evidence submitted to the British Parliament, amounting to many volumes, that there is more maiming of the human body, and more crushing of the human mind, from infancy to the grave, in the manufactories of Great Britain, by the cruelties inflicted on that perpetual bondage which in fact endures from generation to generation, than the *whole amount* of the same class of evils inflicted on *all* the slaves in the United States, notwithstanding the immense difference between the number of persons in one case and the other; and that this result may be established by the best certified evidence. If it should be said, that the bondage of the British manufactories is voluntary, we reply, *it is not*, and that the *law of necessity* which imprisons its victims there, while they can work, on a bare subsistence, without enough to get away, and dismisses them when they can work no longer, without providing for their support, is far more cruel than American bondage, where the law that makes it hereditary, provides for the sick and superannuated. We are quite aware, that one of these cases does not justify, though it relieves, the other, by the light of comparison. There is no state of society in the world, not even in the free States of North America, where these cruelties and inhumanities cannot be found in great abundance. And why do not the Abolitionists begin at home, and tear down society in their respective Commonwealths, because these enormities are to be found, notwithstanding the law and public opinion are against them, in the same manner as law and opinion are against them in the slaveholding States? Or, since they have a propensity to these foreign missions, why do they not go to the nations of Europe, where bondage is more cruel, and where they might, in that proportion, be more useful, if, peradventure, they are likely to be useful at all? In all these cases, and in all parts of the world, these cruelties are exceptions to the general state of society, not the rule.

The decrease of the slave population of the West Indies, and the better economy—barbarous indeed—of keeping it up by importation, was adduced in evidence of the inhumanities of the system. And we think very fairly so. By the same rule, the rapid increase of the slave population in the Southern States, over the whites in the same States—it being in the proportion of 80 to 100 of the whites, and of 112 to 100 of the slaves, in the term of 40 years—proves, that slavery in the United States is comparatively mild. It is commonly reported and believed, by disinterested visitants to the slave States of the Union, that, from all appearances, the slaves, as a body, are the happiest people in the world. And although we are far from advocating the doctrine, in application to involuntary and hereditary bondage, as an element of society, that, "where ignorance is bliss, 'tis folly to be wise;" yet the real condition of American slavery, when fairly ascertained, may go to show, that the pains taken by Abolitionists, in the use of false testimony, to awaken a romantic sympathy in the North, and to muster and urge on a violent crusade upon the South, in violation of the laws of the land, and of the obvious proprieties of man's social condition, thereby disturbing the public peace, and threatening to bring about a civil war, involves a very grave responsibility. It is undoubtedly true, that the Abolitionists of the North know very little about Southern slavery; and that they know far less about it now, than they did before the Abolition press, under the American Anti-Slavery Society, began to instruct them. Nearly all their sympathy is romantic, resting on "the baseless fabric of a vision;" and they may rely upon it, that their crusade upon the South has as little hope of good result, as may now be read in the history of the crusade of the Christian nations of Europe upon "the Holy land."

CHAPTER XI
EVERY MAN MIND HIS OWN BUSINESS

The observance of this rule would secure universal peace. There would never be quarrelling, never war, on the smaller or larger scale; but the breach of it soon produces difficulty, and leads to strife. We have stated in a former chapter, to the effect, that the causes of the Abolition movement of this country, cannot be understood, without allusion to certain cognate events and reforming schemes, that have been set on foot among us, and to certain extravagant and peculiar features of those reforms, which fairly entitle them to the name of *violent*. For example, it was assumed, that the action and scope of Christian benevolence could not stop short of calling all men to account for their principles, manners, habits, and especially meats and drinks, according as these interrogators, *alias* inquisitors, might judge to be wrong. Great Societies were formed to give to these measures the weight and sanction of their publicly declared opinion; and under the shield of Conventional and solemn resolutions, which struck at the root of all independence of private opinion and private character, and excommunicated from good society all that should refuse a strict conformity to these published "Bulls," by stamping them with the *taint* of immorality, their Agents went forth upon the land to deal authoritative rebuke and denunciation against dissentients. The rest is known. All we have to say is, that schools of this kind—and we have only pointed to *one* of many—were admirable preparations for the Abolition movement. A public that would bear all this, it was thought, would bear any thing else; and they who had been accustomed freely, and with little opposition, to use these high prerogatives in the religious and moral sphere, ventured *one* step farther, into the *political*. They did it without scruple, seeming to regard themselves as well entitled to one field, as to the other; and to this day, they seem not to have discovered the impropriety of the trespass.

Now, let it be understood, that the application of these remarks does not go a whit farther, than to comprehend those violent reforms, of which the great body of the religious public of this country, of all denominations, or nearly all, are heartily tired, and earnestly wish them a good riddance. We think we are entitled, without offending any Christian, not an Abolitionist, to point to this indubitable source of this great movement, inasmuch as it would be impossible to do justice to this subject without this leave. It is the wide spread sanction that has been given to *meddling* and *interference* in the social state, and the protracted and almost undisputed use of this prerogative, that has conjured up the spirit of Abolitionism, and given it weight and influence among that class of persons, who sustained the other violent reforms, with few exceptions. They have generally passed readily and regularly, as a matter of course, from one sphere of action to the other, accumulating forces as they advanced. It is even astonishing to observe, how that gem of society, independence of private character, and the right of private opinion, has been marred and prostrated before the authoritative edicts of these high and formidable Associations, the most extravagant of which were concocted in caucus, and forced upon the public, by those very men who will generally be found in the Abolition ranks.

We think it a great mistake, in the administration of the social state, and highly injurious to it, that this title to interfere in the affairs of our neighbors, has been so widely sanctioned. It is bad in itself; and bad in all its results. Once give sanction to this principle by public authority, and there is no end to the modes and forms of its application, in private life or public affairs, in the religious or political world; and there is scarcely any thing more fruitful of strife, or more mischievous in its workings. The reformer assumes, that he has a right, and is bound, to seek the good of his neighbour—*in his own way*, of course—and there is the mistake. And if he can get the sanction of the public, on a large scale, as to the use of his *particular* modes, he is then backed by authority, and is confident. He will then march directly into society, and rebuke and denounce opposition with little ceremony. We are doubtless understood by these allusions. The rule laid down becomes a bed of Procustes: If any one's legs happen to be too long, they must be cut off; or if too short, they must be stretched out by force. And so it goes. There is no such thing as private judgment, private conscience, or independence of character; but a man's soul, and body, and every thing must yield to authority; or, he will have the mark set upon his forehead, and be denounced, as the enemy of society, because he does not agree in opinion with these men, as to the best modes of promoting its interests.

Great and lamentable as the evil of Abolitionism is in our country, and inauspicious in its aspects, we confess, we are not sorry, since it has come to this, that these violent reformers have now got into a position, in which they must encounter an authority that will be likely to rebuke their *meddling interference*, in terms and in a manner which they have not heretofore experienced. Having taken political ground, in violation of the laws of the country, they must henceforth look "the powers that be" in the face, and render an account for their temerity.

CHAPTER XII
PERFECTIONISM

This is a theological term, and announces the doctrine, as we understand it, that it is possible for man to be perfect in this life, and perfect at once. It is a species of *immediatism*; indeed, it is the essence of it, its origin, and foundation; and out of this abstract, theological, and visionary scheme grew the practical and momentous doctrine of *immediate* abolition. This is the application of *perfectionism* to politics, which was originally a religious notion. At all points we see, therefore, that Abolitionism has to do with religion, and religion with it. Whether such an interference of religion with politics, will be agreeable to the people of this country, remains to be seen.

Perfectionism is an old doctrine in the religious world, but has recently been revived in this country, and extensively adopted in the ranks of these violent reformers, whose impatience would not allow them to wait for the action and effect of the ordinary and generally approved means of improving society. With the abstract notion in their heads, that all sin ought to be left off *now*—from which, and so far, we have no inclination to dissent—they have jumped to the conclusion, that it can, must, and shall be; and accordingly have adopted a system of action which assumes, that all departments of society, social, moral, religious, and political, can be managed on this principle.

It will be seen, that the principles of the New England Nonresistance Society, which have been set forth in a former chapter, are the legitimate result of this doctrine. They have stepped at once on the ground of universal anarchy, by renouncing allegiance to all human government, because they say it is badly constituted, and ought to be broken up *instantly*. Nothing wrong in society, they being judges, is to be tolerated for a moment. The entire fabric of society, therefore, being wrong, requires to be dissolved at once. It is fortunate for the public, that in the case of the New England Nonresistance Society, we have a fair exemplification of these principles. *It is perfectionism carried out.* We need go no farther to see what this doctrine, reduced to practice, will lead to.

It may be seen, therefore, *whence* the doctrine of *immediate* Abolition has come, and how it proposes to sweep every thing before it that stands in its way. Like the members of the Nonresistance Society, the Abolitionists are fighting characters. The former declare, "We propose to assail iniquity in *high* places and in low; to apply our principles to *all existing civil, political, legal, and ecclesiastical institutions.*" The Abolitionists differ from this scheme by taking one thing at a time; in that, they are doubtless more wise. But it is precisely the same principle applied in this particular direction.

It will be seen, therefore, that the peace of this country has been disturbed, and the integrity of our political fabric menaced, by a visionary, and we may add, fanatical religious notion. In violation of the Constitutional law of the land, so far as respects the nature of the Abolition organization, as shown in the second chapter and onward, and also in violation of a distinct, established, and well known principle of our Government, to wit, that religion shall not enter into the State, the Abolitionists, as a religious *sect*— for it cannot be denied that such is their character—have marched directly into the political field, with this anarchical principle in hand, and under a vast and powerful political machinery, have assailed the Government of the country, and directly interfered with the Constitutional prerogatives of foreign States. They have solemnly declared, in their highest and most authoritative State paper, the Annual Report of the Society, as before seen, that these Constitutional regulations, defining the prerogatives of the slave States, are null and void, and no longer binding. Of course, it is not to be supposed they will respect them. And will the people of this country allow a *religious* faction to take possession of the Government, and dictate to Sovereign States, with which we are in solemn covenant to protect and defend them in these matters, what they shall do—to *enforce* their principle of *perfectionism* on the political structure of our society, to dissolve and overthrow it?

We do not mean to say, or to intimate, that Abolitionists are all *perfectionists* in the religious sense of this term, and in regard to *all* modes of improving society. That is not true. But we do mean to say, that Abolitionism emanates from this source, and that, like the gradual progress of all error, it is only a stage to the admission of the full sweep of the doctrine. It is a notable fact, however, that the religious perfectionists of the country, who are numerous, are almost to a man Abolitionists, and the most violent of the sect.

It is not necessary to suppose, that perfectionism in the community should have pervaded the entire mass before it can do mischief; or that it cannot have a surreptitious influence on individuals, in regard to particular subjects and in particular applications, while they disclaim the doctrine, and that very sincerely. In this way a man may be an Abolitionist, yet not a perfectionist in general.

The doctrine of perfectionism may be much safer as a theological than as a political notion, for individuals than for society; inasmuch as the religious perfectionist keeps two separate moral reckonings: one for his virtues, the other for his faults. When he happens to be guilty of a fault, he is in a state of *lapse*; at other times in a state of *perfectionism*. We hope his faults are rare; but when he happens to get into them unavoidably, society holds him up. But alas! when society *lapses*, who and what will hold that up? This single question brings the whole subject before the mind's eye, in its political bearings, and suggests the folly and madness of that doctrine, which attempts to introduce perfectionism into the social system.

As the religionist professes respect for the Bible, and for Divine authority, it may be well to refer him to these examples on this particular point. We say, then, that, although God is an *immediatist* in the authoritative force of his law over the conscience of individuals, he is not an immediatist as the Governor of the world. Clearly, it cannot be denied, that God could have made human society perfect *at once*; but for some good reason he has not done so. If it should be replied: "It is because men do not *obey*" — Very well. We speak of a *great fact*, under God's administration of the world. Moreover, if the *Divine* legation of Moses be allowed, we have the authority of the Saviour, that he enacted a certain law of divorcement "for the hardness of their hearts;" that is, as we suppose, on account of the bad state of society, and not because it was right: "for it was not so from the beginning."[8] For the same reason, as *we* hold, though we have not the same authority for saying it, Moses *legalized* slavery. If it was *not* for that reason, then the slave holders have the highest authority for the institution. It is impossible to get off from this dilemma by the plea of *different forms*, while the *principle* stares us in the face. Forms of society are *accidental*, and never agree exactly, and often differ widely, under the same name, in different ages and countries.

[8] Matth. 19: 8. Mark 10: 5.

John the Baptist was a Divinely commissioned teacher. "And the *soldiers* likewise demanded of him, saying, And what shall *we* do?" Though not a member of the New England Nonresistance Society, we are a little bit of a Quaker, and hold that the principles of Christianity are at *war* with war. Consequently, if *immediatism* is to be forced upon society, according to *our* notions, John should have replied: "The first thing, my friends, is to lay down your arms." But, "he said unto them, Do violence to no man; neither accuse any falsely; and be content with your *wages*."

We believe it true to say, that no Divinely commissioned teacher ever attempted to introduce *immediatism* as an element of the social fabric; or ever protested against the action of society for want of it, so long as we understand immediatism to be an attempt to sweep away, by one stroke, every fault, or defect, or imperfection of society. Such was not the example of *Christ*; and such was not the example of the Apostle Paul, in application to slavery itself, as will appear in his courteous treatment of Philemon, a slave-holder. So also in this Apostle's doctrine, and in the doctrine of the Apostle Peter.[9] History proves, that the persons called "servants" in these passages, were slaves, or the property of their masters. Yet the Apostles never felt authorized, or saw fit, to disturb this state of society, bad as it was in this particular, and many others; but they availed themselves of the facilities afforded them by the existence of political society to apply *immediatism* to the consciences of individuals, in regard to the state of their hearts, and to their personal conduct.

[9] I Cor. 7: 20, 21. I Tim. 6: 1, 2. Eph. 6: 5, 9. Titus 2: 9, 10. Coloss. 3: 22, and 4: 1. I Pet. 2: 18, 20.

If, indeed, the Abolitionists will produce a *Divine* commission, sustained by miracles, entitling them to go *one step* farther than any other Divinely commissioned teachers have ever gone, by investing them with authority to *remodel* political society, we will respect their claim, and advise the public to do so. But till that time, we think it fair to say, that the *preaching* of such doctrines as they choose to maintain, moral, social, religious, or political, *independent of any political organization*, such as they *now* have, to sustain them, is all they are entitled to by the Constitution and laws of this land. By *preaching*, we mean, of course, to comprehend all the *prescribed* Constitutional modes of political action, so long as they choose to meddle with politics. Preaching to *private* conscience, is one thing; and that is the office of Christianity, within the range of its own precepts. But the political constitution and administration of society, is another thing; and this, in *our* opinion, Christianity never presumes to meddle with.

CHAPTER XIII
LIBERTY AND EQUALITY

Aware, that we are constantly liable to perversion as to the intent of our remarks in these pages, it is proper for us to say, that we have not taken up this topic in order to bring our interpretation of it to bear against the right of slaves to their freedom. That is a question which we do not assume to discuss, though we have signified our opinion, and are ready freely and frankly so to do on all proper occasions. But our object at this time is to correct the vague, poetic, and romantic notions which are commonly attached to these terms. In this country, their origin may fairly be ascribed to a notable declaration, so often quoted from our national bill of rights: "that all men are created equal, and that they are endowed by their Creator with certain unalienable rights, among which are life, liberty, and the pursuit of happiness." Now, what is the meaning of this? The history of those times, and of the occasions which produced it, will answer this question.

First, as to the term *Liberty*. The British Government refused the Colonies a representation in the law-making power of the empire, and this was the ground of the quarrel, the cause of the Revolution. We have, then, in this great historical fact, a fair and clear interpretation of the meaning of the term "liberty" in the declaration of Rights, viz. the right to a representation of the people in the law-making authority. So much and no more, we conceive, is the meaning of this term in this place; and that is enough for the free and full action of "the principles of our republican form of Government." In connexion with the provisions of our National and State Constitutions, the people are thus constituted the law-making power. That is, they are entitled to *govern* themselves. But the very idea of Government is *subjection* to law, not a *liberty* for every man to do as he pleases. This last meaning is the *vague, poetic,* and *romantic* notion commonly attached to this term — to do as one pleases; whereas, the Constitutional and proper meaning is the *right* to a voice in the making of law. In the strict sense of the term, therefore, it is not liberty, but a right. The moment a man enters into society, he resigns his liberty, and consents to be *subjected* to the regulations of the community, of which he is a member. There is no liberty, except in the simple state of nature, where man is isolated from man, and becomes a solitary savage.

Having alluded to *the state of nature*, it may be proper in this place to observe, that the same poetic fancies are constantly played off on "natural rights," as on liberty and equality; whereas, the slightest reflection ought to teach us, that all society is artificial and conventional, and that no man who enters into society can any farther lay claim to "natural rights" than the law allows. Every regulation of society is so far an infringement on natural rights, if, indeed, we have any correct notion of the meaning of these terms. It is difficult, indeed, to define natural rights. We have never yet seen it done, and confess our own inability for the task. What is the use, then, in talking about that for which we cannot find even a definition? We have a right, however, since it is used for practical purposes, to make it mean something. Say, then, that it means such rights as a savage would be entitled to, when alone in the desert, to do what he is inclined, as in such circumstances he would not interfere with any social right. But in society men give up their natural rights, if the above is a fair statement of what they are; and the law becomes the rule of right. The whole system of society is artificial, and at war with natural rights; and he who claims the privilege of natural right, in opposition to the established code of society, asserts the right of rebellion. We have no objection, however, that any body should give us a definition of natural rights, that would lead to a different conclusion, if it can be done; but till that time, we are compelled to say, that this talk about natural rights, for any practical purpose in society, is something we do not understand, unless, for example, it be the right to live and to breathe; and even that may be forfeited to the law. Suppose the murderer sentenced to be hung, should claim the privilege of natural rights—would he be heard? Natural rights, as we understand them, are not available in society, when they interfere with law. That is to say, the law is always above them, and must be, so long as it is judged best to maintain the social state. There is not a single natural right that can be named, which may not, in given cases, be abridged, or controlled, or superseded, or entirely suppressed, by the artificial organisation of society. To talk of natural right, therefore, as being paramount to law, simply because it *is* natural right, is arrant nonsense—mere declamation, at best.

But, to return to "liberty." We have seen, that the Constitutional meaning of this term in our Charter or Bill of rights is limited to the single and simple claim to a voice by representation in the power of making law, and that laws are made for our *subjection*. All the rest beyond this is *duty*, *obedience, not* liberty. Law limits and circumscribes us at all points, in the house and out of it, every where, in relation to every body, and to every body's rights. All the rights of our fellow beings, as secured by law, are an abridgment of our liberty. The higher the degrees of civilization, which add to the multiplication of laws, so much greater is the abridgment of liberty. That is, the more perfect society is made, so much less of liberty do we have; and, as good citizens, we are not only contented with it, but we prefer it. For the advantages of society, we enter into terms of mutual concession; and every degree of concession cuts us off from liberty.

Now for the romance of "Equality"—"that all men are created *equal.*" And what is the meaning of this in the Charter of our rights? Simply, that royal blood, and noble blood, is no better than any other blood; and therefore, that we will have no king, and no aristocracy. The hereditary and divine right of kings, and the hereditary right of nobles, are here barred, and the *people* are enthroned in their place, with all the chances open before them of *rising* in society, according to their merits, even to the highest honors of the Republic. This, we think, is the exact meaning of equality in this place, and that it goes no farther than to cut off the hereditary claims of kings and nobles, and of privileged orders in the community—that is, of orders privileged by the enactments of Constitutional law. But this principle, obviously, was never intended to apply practically to general society, nor to any ranks of society below these degrees. In this sense of the term the whole community is reduced fairly to what is generally understood by the republican level: that all may have a chance to rise according to their merits. But who will say, that it was intended to make a President of the United States of a man, who has no sort of qualification or claim to that office? Or to raise any man to an honor or office, to which he is not judged to be entitled by a majority of those voices appointed by law to determine such a question? Who will say, that it was intended to annihilate those grades of society, which the use of common rights necessarily creates, because one man is more industrious, or more virtuous, or more fortunate than another? Who will say, that it was intended to establish the Agrarian principle, that because the industry of one man has built him a good house, the lazy, idle, and worthless man has a right to claim a part of it, and a part of the wealth of its owner? Or, that all inequalities of wealth and condition in life, produced by different degrees of virtue, application to business, and good luck, are to be levelled by making all things common, and an equal distribution to every man, whatever may be his character? We are disposed to believe, that our American society is hardly yet prepared for the application of such a rule as this; or that there is a single man in the community who will relinquish his fairly acquired rights and property to those, who may happen not to have acquired the same advantages.

As a matter of fact, there is no such thing as equality among men, nor can there be. There is no equality in their physical powers, none in the circumstances of their birth and education, none in the privileges and wealth which they inherit or acquire, none in their social advantages—*no* equality in any thing. The two men cannot be found who are in all or any respects exactly equal. If all the talents and powers of the whole community were solely devoted to produce equality, they would be unequal to the task. Neither God nor man ever instituted equality. We do not say, that God could not have done it; but, to our taste, he would have spoiled creation, if he had. We desire, therefore, and think we have good reasons, to be contented with such a Universe as he has made. We desire also to be contented, that any man, by his virtues or good fortune, should be more elevated and better off than ourself. If we are not, we sin: "Thou shalt not covet." This Divine law, was enacted for such a case, as well as others; and the very frame of society was intended to maintain these inequalities; that is, to secure to every man his own rights.

What, then, becomes of this *song* of liberty and equality—this poetry and romance of popular declamation—this soul-stirring and heaven-appealing claim?—Has nothing really been acquired? Yes, much: We have acquired the right of making our own laws, and cut off kings and nobles from all claim to hereditary ascendancy. This is a great, a mighty achievement, if we prove wise enough to know how to use it. We hold it to be an advance in human society—a most important acquisition to the liberties and rights of mankind. But it will be seen, that the general and vague notion commonly attached to these terms is utterly without foundation—mere poetry and romance.

We may ask, then, with what propriety the Abolitionists apply this passage in our National bill of rights to slavery? Obviously, there is no warrant for it, if we stick to the meaning and intent thereof. If they see fit to give it another meaning—to force a construction from it that was never intended, of course, in such an arbitrary interpretation, we can have no farther controversy with them, than to state, that it *is* arbitrary.

We deem it proper to say, that the Bill of Rights set forth in the Declaration of our Independence, was never intended for such an application; but that this particular passage was limited to the two single points which we have noticed. It neither affirms nor denies, it neither vitiates nor strengthens, the claim of the slave to his freedom, because it never contemplated the case. We are now settling a question of fact. To be wrong is one thing; to be inconsistent another. That there is wrong in slavery we do not deny; but we do say, that there is no inconsistency in the existence of slavery in the United States with our National Bill of Rights, when fairly interpreted. It will doubtless be allowed, that the Federal Constitution is a good interpreter of that Bill; and that decrees the perpetuity of slavery, at the will of the slave States. The *consistency* of our Government, and of our country, therefore, is maintained and defended, in this particular, against all imputation to the contrary, whatever may be the *right* of the case. If any body chooses to say, that the *principle* involved in this passage of our Bill of Rights *reaches* the case of the slave, we have no objection. For, we frankly confess, we have always thought so too. But we deny, that it was ever intended to have such an application, and that there is any inconsistency, however there may be wrong, in the existence of slavery in our country, so long as we abide by the Bill of Rights and the Constitution as the rule, when interpreted according to their meaning.

We gained a great step in the acquisition of our National Independence; but we did not arrive to a state of *perfectionism*. Since that time we have made advances in society, for the better, too. We have abolished the slave trade, and slavery itself in all the States north of Mason's and Dixon's line; and it is manifest, that the slave States bordering on the free, are greatly affected by the influence of the latter, to make slave property less valuable, and to lead towards emancipation. But so long as the laws of the land are respected and maintained, the slave States can never be compelled to emancipation by foreign dictation; nor will they be advised. By the existing regulations of society, there is no power authorized to advise them. We, of the North, in like circumstances, would not be advised. Every State and nation is the best judge of what may be expedient in the management of its own domestic polity; and if any of its component parts are depressed and oppressed, they have an undoubted right to relieve themselves, if they can, at their own risk. But the law of nations, which is the highest and most important of all laws, and the breach of which is most momentous in its consequences, does not authorize, but forbids, interference.

CHAPTER XIV
SOCIAL AND POLITICAL EFFECTS
OF ABOLITIONISM

First, its *social* effects. It has produced a very unhappy state of feeling in the North. Just in proportion to a man's unreasonableness, if he happens to be in the wrong, will be his zeal to maintain his cause; and the effect of his zeal on all concerned may generally be measured by the same rule. The Abolitionists are believed to be in the wrong; and the extreme zeal and infatuation, not to say madness, with which they urge their cause, would seem to prove them so. Why should men, conscious of the rectitude of their principles and conduct, be violent? Even if they were in the heat of battle, dignity and self possession, and even generosity towards their foes, would be more becoming. That they are the aggressors, is certain. Who else began it? Like as a man, who slanders his neighbour, will take all possible pains to prove it is not slander, and by-and-by believe his own story, because he has told it so often, and is determined to have it so; so the Abolitionists, becoming fervid in their cause, persuade themselves that they are right. But they appear to the rest of the community so unreasonable, and so manifestly wrong, that the effect of their zeal on the public mind is very unhappy—more especially so, as the interests of the country, which are dear to all good citizens, are put in great peril by their movement. Hence families, neighbourhoods, towns, cities, and the whole community, are divided, and driven to acrimonious controversy on this subject. We scarcely recollect any occasion of public excitement in this country, that has given birth to greater violence of language, to more uncharitableness, or greater bitterness of feeling, than this. That this bad temper has been all on one side, it would be unjust to say; but that the Abolitionists have had a good share of it, we think it no libel to suggest; nor are we prepared to say, that they have endured opposition in the most Christian-like way. We hesitate not to say, that their literary publications are of a very inflammatory character. Even the grave and solemn document of their last Annual Report—or which ought to have been grave and solemn—is so rude, violent, and denunciatory—so much like a tear-all-down—that the nerves of a well composed person, as we will venture to say, will be not a little *dis*-composed in the reading thereof. One is shocked to think, that we have come to such revolutionary times, as that production would seem to indicate—that a grand political organization, wielding such a tremendous sway of influence, as the American Anti-Slavery Society, should take upon itself to declare the Constitutional law of the land null and void, and no longer binding; and by one stroke of the pen to abrogate the authority of the Senate of the Nation, and proclaim their decisions as worthy only of contempt. What next? But we forbear; for we seem to feel, that we are getting into the same strain, inasmuch as the record of the simple facts of their history is too exciting to be set in their true light. No wonder then, that the people of this country have felt themselves injured and outraged by such bold assaults on that social edifice, under the shadow, and within the precincts of which, they have and hold all their most valuable privileges. It is a pity, indeed, that fellow citizens and christian brethren should be driven so far asunder, and be filled with so much animosity, by such an unnatural broil. On whom does this responsibility rest? In our judgment, on those who have instigated the quarrel, on the aggressors, and not on those who act merely on the defensive, in vindication and support of the Government of the country. The question, now, is not the rights of the slave; that is entirely set aside by another, which this controversy has forced into its place—the peace of the country, and the integrity of the Union.

But the social effects between the North and the South are much more unhappy, than between the Abolitionists and Anti-Abolitionists of the North. Time was when a northern man could go to the South without suspicion, and be received in all good faith. But it is no longer so. The very name of a Northerner is odious at the South, till his personal qualities shall happen to make him agreeable. Time was, when a Southern man could enjoy himself in visiting the North, and be honored; but now he feels, that every second man he meets with may be an Abolitionist, to him a name of horror, because he loves his wife and his children, and thinks of the terrible scenes which the doctrines and measures of the Abolitionists expose them to. In the social intercourse of the North with the South, there has been raised a barrier of a very formidable character, and every month and every day it is getting worse and worse. It is impossible it should be otherwise, so long as the end of this sad controversy cannot be foreseen.

The violence of language used by the Abolitionists against the slave States and slave holders, is most uncharitable and unwarrantable, and its social effects pernicious. The people of the South are *men*, and remarkable for their courtesy and hospitality to strangers. They have been educated to think and to feel, that slavery is justifiable in the circumstances under which it has come down to them. They do not view the subject as we Northerners do. And admitting that they are wrong, the worst that could be said of them is, that they are unenlightened in this particular. They are found to be gentlemen, amiable and kind, and many of them Christians—yes, Christians. Philemon, of Bible notoriety, was a Christian, and a slaveholder. And yet the Abolitionists do not hesitate to call them MONSTERS in human shape!

But the *political* effects are still worse, in so far as they are more important and more momentous. Abolition is a fire brand on the floor of Congress, which we have reason to fear is gratifying to the movers of this sedition. But the worst of all is, the South is evidently anticipating and preparing for a dissolution of the Union; and no spirit of prophecy, now the gift of mortals, can foretell the consequences of such an event. If it shall be forced by this agitation, one of the first measures of the South will be to visit with tremendous vengeance all disturbers of their peace in this particular concern; and who of us, in like circumstances, could blame them for it? And the misfortune will be, that the innocent will not always escape, as every Northern man will of course be suspected. Would it not be difficult to maintain peace between two such Republics? Evidently, nothing is more to be deprecated in a political horoscope, than a dissolution of this Union. The South is essential to the North, and the North to the South, on the terms of the Federal compact; but put them asunder, by such a cause, and the chances are, that they will be implacable enemies. To all these evils are we exposed by the Abolition movement, besides what have already come.

CHAPTER XV
THE BAD EFFECTS OF ABOLITIONISM ON THE FREE COLORED POPULATION, AND ON THE CONDITION AND PROSPECTS OF SLAVES

It cannot be denied, that Abolitionism has created a very unpleasant state of feeling in the minds of the free colored population, and made them unhappy; that it has excited them, in no inconsiderable degree, to insubordination as citizens; that it has vitiated their domestic and social character, as servants, wherever they are employed; that it has invested them with an importance, in their own esteem, which the present state of society is not prepared to award them, and encouraged them to assume airs which are often rebuked to their great unhappiness, and to the disturbance and injury of their temper; and that it has exposed them to insult and outrage from the lower classes of the white population, which very naturally provokes the same kind of treatment in return, and consequently keeps alive perpetual feuds in these conditions of life, not unfrequently leading to tragical results, in which generally the colored people have the worst of it.

It will be observed, that we are now stating facts, not principles. Abolitionists may say, it ought not to be so, and we admit it. But their error is, in this, as in all departments of their cause, that they build and go on the principle of *perfectionism*, and refuse to submit to the suggestions of practical wisdom—of experience. They assume, that it is possible to manage society just as if it were perfect in its structure, and morally perfect in all its component parts, and insist, that it shall be so managed. The consequence is, that disturbance instantly insues, on the attempt to enforce their principles, and the colored people are doomed to suffer the evil consequences of the rashness of their pretended friends and benefactors, besides that they are injured in their temper and character as citizens.

Again we observe, that we are stating facts, as we know that we are exposed to misrepresentation. We say, then, what every body knows— though we regret the fact as sincerely as any one can—that the free colored people of this country, with few exceptions, have risen, in person or by genealogy, from a depressed condition, from a state of bondage, which, in connexion with the public feeling and prejudice against the race, on account of a difference of physical constitution, subjects them unfortunately to social disadvantage, in a white population, who have always had the ascendency, and to whom society, as it exists, owes its origin and maintenance. This may be wrong in the widest view and with the most generous construction of human rights, as they are commonly maintained in the abstract; but it is a fact. We say, moreover, in reference to such a fact, it has never been known, in the history of human society, that such a class has risen, by a single step, to a full equality of social immunity and privilege. We know it is a doctrine of *perfectionism*, but it is not a practicable doctrine, in our opinion. It will doubtless commonly be regarded as impossible for such a class to be qualified, except by time and degrees, for such a station in society with a white population. To attempt, therefore, to enforce it on the people of this country, in such circumstances, is only to make the colored people unhappy, to put a claim into their mouths which they cannot hope to realize, and to arm the white population with still stronger prejudices against them.

Look, for example, to the effect of the Abolition agitation, in the formation and adoption of the new Constitution of the State of Pennsylvania: Before, free colored people, of specific qualifications, were entitled to the privilege of electors; now they are all disfranchised. We are inclined to the opinion, that if all the Northern States were now engaged in remodelling their Constitutions—especially where the colored people are numerous—they would do the same thing, merely as the effect of the Abolition movement. However this may be regretted, it is a natural consequence, and on the Abolitionists rests the responsibility. Just in proportion as they violently urge their measures, will the social privileges of the colored population be abridged, and their comfort, happiness, and prospects impaired. Before this agitation commenced, the colored people were comparatively contented and happy, their privileges were being extended, they were gradually rising in the scale of society, and every body—at least the public generally—were gratified to see them rise, and ready to help them. There was a common pleasure in encouraging the worthy and industrious of their color; and though an Abolitionist may be surprised at the fact, *we* have entertained them *as guests* in our house, and at our table for days in succession, in the same manner and with the same hospitalities which we are accustomed to render to those of our own color, and with much greater satisfaction, because we were delighted to see such proofs of their excellence and worth. And notwithstanding that the measures of the Abolitionists have thrown formidable obstacles in the way, we declare, we would do the same thing again, in like circumstances. But however worthy they may be, and the more worthy they are, they would be backward and diffident in accepting such hospitalities, simply because the effect of the Abolition movement has been to depress, instead of raising them in society. It has abridged their privileges at all points, and in all their relations with the white population, the Abolitionists only excepted. Nor can the favor of the Abolitionists be regarded as a fair and full indemnification for the loss they have sustained by such an unfortunate alliance, inasmuch as the highest and most influential agencies of society are now, and are likely to continue, indirectly armed against them, by maintaining the Government, and defending the institutions of the country, against violence. The effect of the agitation, generally and particularly, on the colored people themselves, and on the white population individually and collectively, is to abridge the privileges of the former, and to injure them.

We are aware, that the Abolitionists will probably say, such incidental and unavoidable evils are always the concomitants of great reformations in society. We suppose, of course, they will not say, it is a proof of the justice of their cause, as such a reason would go to authorize any mischief. These facts, then, are admitted. Indeed, we see not, how they can be denied. It remains to be seen, whether the final result will be any better than the beginning. We fear it will not.

But the effects of Abolitionism on the condition and prospects of the slaves, is even and far worse than on the free colored people. It has rivetted the chains of slavery with a manifold firmness and strength; it has greatly abridged the privileges before allowed them for intellectual and moral culture; it has barred the door, in the slave States, against all open and free discussion of the subject of emancipation, which before was tolerated; it has interdicted all intercourse between the North and South, that presumes to meddle with the subject of slavery, and of course raised an insurmountable barrier against the social influence of the North in this particular direction; it has barred the influence of public opinion on slavery from all quarters beyond the slave States; it has driven the South as a body to maintain the *principle* of slavery *out* and *out*, without restriction or qualification, whereas before, a large portion of the slave-holders were ready to admit it was wrong, desired to see their way out of it, and were open to advice; it has caused to be established a most rigid police and surveillance over the system; it has multiplied the enactments and increased the strength of legislation for its protection and defence; it has nerved the arm of the law with greater vigor and determination; it has bound the slave States together by stronger ties in defence of a common interest; it has given sanction to Lynch law for the summary treatment of offenders; and for all these, and many other reasons that might be named, it has put far off the day of emancipation, if it has not determined the *perpetuity* of slavery.

Here, again, the Abolitionists will perhaps say, it only proves the right of our cause, and that all this is the struggle of a last and dying effort. But, it might be wise for them not to forget, that the bulwark of the Nation's Constitution stands between them and slavery; and that, till that is pulled down and trampled under foot, as they themselves have set the example in their last Annual Report, they will not have gained their object. Nay, though the fabric of the Nation should be broken in pieces by their hands, and thrown to the winds of Heaven, such is the spirit they have kindled in the South, that they would be compelled to wade through blood, and with iron heel to trample on the carcasses of their opponents, before they will have triumphed. We speak of men as they are, as they always have been, and as they are likely for some time yet to be; and in doing so, the language we employ is no figure of speech, but, as we think, the veritable prophecy of the future. And by the time the Abolitionists shall have done this work, there will be good room and a fit opportunity for the establishment of a despotism unrivalled in severity by any known to the present age, as the only adequate remedy for the anarchy they will have produced.

Such are some of the lamentable effects of this lamentable movement, as they bear on the free coloured people, and on the condition and prospects of the slaves of this country; and we submit them to the serious consideration of those whom it may concern.

CHAPTER XVI
A HYPOTHETICAL VIEW OF ABOLITIONISM

We think it must strike every intelligent observer—every one certainly that lays claims to any knowledge in the workings of society—that *immediate* Abolition, whenever acquired by the measures now in operation—admitting it can be effected without a civil war, though we do not believe it can—must find the two conflicting parties in the worst possible humour in relation to each other. On the one side would be arrayed the Abolitionists with their protégés; and on the other the party defeated after a long and violent struggle. In the mean time all the colored people, now free or in bondage, will have been filled with the most violent hatred and animosity towards the opponents of their claims. The feeling already produced in that class of colored people, that has come under the influence of Abolitionists, may serve as an illustration; and the well known principles of human nature may fill out the complement of the lesson. It would be seen by the people of this country, in the progress of events, long before this object shall have been attained, that an immediate emancipation at any time, brought about by such means, will place the country in a most undesirable and perilous condition. These anticipations and apprehensions must necessarily, as we think, mount to an insuperable barrier.—Self-preservation is the first law of nature; and when that comes to be the question, either with individuals or with society, people are not wont to suspend action to discuss casuistry or right.—The drowning man seizes the plank within his reach, even though he should hear the voice of a remonstrant, giving some very subtle reasons why he ought not to do so. So society, finding itself in peril, from within or from without, will save itself, if it can. We are inclined to believe, that the harder Abolition is pushed in its present shape, and under its present avowed principles, so much greater will be the apprehensions of the people, as to the consequences of its success. We think they will never consent, that three millions of the colored race should be raised by one step, from the condition in which they now are, to a full equality of privilege with all other citizens, backed by such a party as the Abolitionists, and actuated by their principles. The dangers would be too obvious and too imminent to admit of parley. They must first be made to believe in *perfectionism*, before they would venture on such an experiment. Every stage of the progress of Abolitionism hitherto, instead of allaying those apprehensions, has only served to augment them. If the peace of the country can hardly be maintained now, and is more and more disturbed at every successive stage of the movement, under its present organization, who can answer for it a little while to come?—Much more, who could answer for it in the hottest of the conflict? The Abolitionists insist on principles, apart from emancipation, which rouse popular indignation, and occasionally blow it into flame, even while the people know that the power is in their own hands. But when once they shall be obliged to see, that these principles are actually going into practice by force, throughout the length and breadth of the land, it requires no prophet to foretell how they will feel, and how they will act. Honestly, we do not think it among the possible events of the future, that Abolition principles, as they now stand forth before the public, can be forced upon the people of this country; but on the contrary, that, foreseeing the evil, they will take care to prevent it.

The Abolitionists cannot appeal to the effects of emancipation in the British West Indies, even on the ground of their own showing, to allay these apprehensions; for there is no parallel between the two cases. Every circumstance and every attribute of the question, as it exists here, in its essential influences, are at variance with that example.

But so long as our political fabric remains such as it is, it would seem to be folly to discuss this subject on this hypothetical basis. We have only taken this license for a moment, for the sake of showing, that, if this political structure of our society were all out of the way, and if the slave-holders had no interest or voice in the question, the avowed principles of the Abolitionists, apart from the difficulty of political rights, would erect an insuperable barrier in the public mind to the accomplishment of their designs.

CHAPTER XVII
ABOLITIONISM CONSIDERED AS PROPOSING NO COMPENSATION FOR SLAVE-PROPERTY

The political frame of society governs the world, the doctrines of *perfectionists* to the contrary notwithstanding; and we shall be heartily thankful that it is so, until we can fall into better hands than this visionary fraternity. And since the Abolitionists have come into the political field, it might be wise for them to consider, whether they can carry their measures in contempt of established political principles. The responsibility of slavery is divided among the community of nations; and there are few of those which profess respect for the code of international law, and feel obliged by their political relations to regard it, that have not some share in it, directly or indirectly. Among these exceptions, if there is any, is the Government of the United States. For we have seen, that it has never made itself responsible for the slavery of individual States. We have also seen, that the slave States are not responsible for its introduction, but that it was imposed upon them by authority. And before the public conscience of the parties concerned had become alive to the enormities and guilt of the slave trade, and much more before slavery itself had become the subject of public remonstrance, it had attained to a growth in the Southern States, not easily to be eradicated. So long, therefore, as political society is dominant, and is bound together by common ties, by common interests, and by common principles, no part of such society can claim of another part the relinquishment of property in slaves without an indemnification. This principle, it will be observed, does not vitiate the claim of the slave to his own freedom; it only affects the parties concerned in the political structure of general society.

The British Government acquitted itself honorably on this point, in decreeing the abolition of slavery in its West India Colonies, and voted a full indemnification for the property, the right to which was thus effaced from the statute book. We say, a *full* indemnification, notwithstanding it is commonly rated higher, as quoted in this country. The reason of this high quotation results from the fact, that it is not commonly considered, perhaps not known, that slave property in the British West Indies had depreciated so greatly and so rapidly in a few years, by political aspects having a bearing upon it, as to have passed, in very large amounts, into other hands, at the depreciated price, by the necessities of bankruptcy, and consequently graduated the valuation of all such property in the same circumstances. Whenever, therefore, that property should be transferred to other holders for any purpose whatever, the commercial valuation at the time would of course be assumed as the rule of estimate. That was the rule consulted by the British Parliament, and it was considered, that the 20,000,000 sterling was a fair estimate of the property redeemed. But, whether this be the exact truth or not, the principle of indemnification was recognized, and was supposed to have been honorably respected in this transaction.

Clearly, it must be seen, that by the political history of the world, and the action of general society, under the sanction of which all those commercial transactions have been carried on, which have determined and graduated the valuation of slave property from time to time, in all and any States where it exists, the public faith of the world that has sanctioned and tolerated slavery so long, and thereby profited by it, is pledged as the guardian of that property to the indemnification of the holders, whenever the public conscience shall demand it to be annihilated, as to its previous form, and return to that law which generally prevails in human society. There is not a man, woman, or child, in the circle of Christendom, hardly in the world, that has not profited by slavery, in a commercial point of view, which is the only point we are here concerned to notice. Much less is there one such individual in the free States of our country, that has not profited by it. All the property of the Northern States, and all their commercial interests, have been interwoven with it. It is that property which has determined the value of ours, and ours that has determined the value of that, reciprocally. And just in proportion to the foreign commercial relations and transactions of our country, does the same rule apply to the respective communities with which we have maintained such intercourse. The amount of the slave property of the South is not theirs, except in the convenient title of a regulation of general society; but it is the world's, or all that part of the world's, where commercial transactions have determined its estimate. But since it has been convenient for the world, for general society, that it should *vest* in certain persons, in the same manner as any other property vests in certain other persons, either here or there, in this country or any other, and that no persons should have any other title in any other property than that which is held by this conventional rule for general good, it would be a manifest and flagrant injustice, robbery, for one part of general society to demand of another part, to resign this title without indemnification, while the party making this demand claims to hold its own. Of course, this question does not touch the right of the slave to himself, or in any way affect that claim.

It may be seen, then, how this matter stands in the United States. We strike at the very foundations of society, when we use our influence to impair the rights of property, as established by general consent; and the impulse of the blow, in the circle of its action, must necessarily return to ourselves, in its natural, or rather artificial, channel, as society in all its parts is an artificial edifice. We can no more move upon the South for such an object, than they can move upon us; in laying our hand upon their property to impair its title, we impair our own in the same degree. For our convenience and profit, be it known, the title to slave property has happened to vest in them; and for their convenience and profit the title to our property has happened to vest in us, because we happen to be here and not there, and they there and not here. Both titles are equally sacred in the relations we bear to each other.

Unless, therefore, the Abolitionists have made up their minds to go into this field in the character of pirates and brigands, we see not how they can move an inch, till they are prepared to make the tender of indemnification for the release of the property which they claim. We aver solemnly, that it is with pain we have written the last sentence, and that if any other terms would have represented the exact truth of the case, as it stands before our mind, we should have preferred them. We agree with the Abolitionists as to the *wrong* of slavery, though we dissent from them, both as to the expediency and duty of *immediate* emancipation, in view of all the facts and circumstances of the case; and we dissent from them utterly, *ab imo pectore*, as to the *validity* of slave property, not in relation to the slave, however, but in relation to general society; and we are prepared to go with the nation for redemption by a fair indemnification. Though we may have little at stake in such a concern, yet he who has little may feel the burden more than he that has much. We are prepared, however, to point out a way, the burden of which no man will feel, and one that is practicable, too. To enforce abolition without indemnification, would be as bad for the slave, as for the master, because it would be the ruin of both; it would blot from future history all those political Commonwealths, because they would be absolutely too poor to maintain themselves.

The most formidable difficulty of Abolitionism, therefore, and the most disorganizing principle, of all, plants itself on the very threshold of the enterprise: *non-indemnification*. Their only reason, so far as we understand, is, that indemnification would be a tacit and implied confession on the *right* of slavery. Admitting, that Abolitionists themselves think and feel so; the rest of the public do not; Abolitionists, therefore, would neither be weakened in principle, nor injured in fact, by giving up this point, except in the workings of their own imagination. This can be a valid objection only as it vitiates principle before the eyes of the public, and in the view of opponents. That, however, not being the fact, the objection ought to lose its force. But suppose some mischievous wags *should* say to the Abolitionists: "Well, gentlemen, you have given up a main principle, after all"—as they would be intitled to make declaration of their reason for consenting to indemnification, they would not only be defended on that point, but receive credit for making a concession, that involves no sacrifice of principle, for the public good. Consent to indemnification, either for one reason or for another—and every man may have his own reason—and one of the principal causes of the contest is superseded. But will the Abolitionists, from sheer stubbornness, insist upon a point, which, if carried, will ruin the slave States, and reduce them to beggary, involving in the catastrophe the ruin of the slaves; upon a point, which levels its blow at the foundation stone of the fabric of society, as it has heretofore existed; upon a point, which, unless human nature be miraculously changed, can never, no never, be gained, without the effusion of blood, no one can tell how much, or what state of things may succeed? Let that point be once properly adjusted, as it may be without compromitting the principles of either party, and much, very much will be gained towards pacification. It is not unlikely, indeed, that the zeal of some engaged in the cause, when they shall find that they may be required to put their hands in their pockets, will be somewhat cooled. And is it not reasonable to suppose also, that some other men's zeal will be somewhat sharpened, when they shall find what will be to them—without imputing any such motives to the aggressors—a horde of bandits at their doors to rob them of their all?

But it may possibly be said, "We do not exactly see how the giving up of slave property, without indemnification, will be the ruin of the slave States." Then we think it must be for the want of eyes.

The value of all capital is commercial, and accidental, and depends on the ever shifting conditions of political society. This may be seen and illustrated by the fluctuating price of that species of capital, called stocks, which is to be found in the market of every civilized community. The price of stocks never makes a false report, as to the political aspects of society, but is as infallible a guage in this particular, as is the thermometer of the weather; and the wise statesman understands it. The same principle which determines the value of this species of capital, determines the value of every other. It only happens that the guage of one is always visible, and that of the others invisible, until they come into market.

The moment emancipation for the British West Indies began to be agitated, the value of slave and other property connected with it, began to fall, and continued to fall, till the certainty of the event reduced it to about one third of what it would otherwise have been, at which time it was redeemed by the British Government at the commercial valuation. It was only public faith in the Government which kept it from going down to nothing; and *this nothing* would of course have been the ruin of the former state of society. What might succeed to such a revolution, would have depended on contingencies which no human foresight could solve beforehand, as every thing would have required to be erected on a new basis. It is a new basis even as it is, but saved from the wreck of a revolution by the care of the British Government; and it is to be hoped, that the wise counsels and strong arm of that Government will make it do well. It is, however, to be observed, that the actual depreciation of slave and other property in the British West Indies, during and in consequence of the Abolition agitation, was so much loss to the individual holders during that period, it being 40,000,000 sterling in slave property alone, if the price of redemption be assumed to have been *one-third* of the hypothetical estimate. It may, possibly, be said, that this is imaginary; but the only sure criterion is the commercial value at any given time, which is always the true value.

In the same manner, the slave property of the southern States, and other portions of their wealth necessarily connected with it, will sink instantly, whenever it shall be seen that the Abolition movement is likely to break down the only protection which it has; and the wealth of the slave States will dwindle, and continue to dwindle, so long as there is any uncertainty in their political prospects arising from such a cause, and in exact proportion to the degree of that uncertainty. This is a principle, a law of society, that is sure to prevail over all other laws, because it is the concentrated action of the entire machinery of society on a single point for the time being, and so far as occasion calls, resulting not from the force of legislation directly— though it may be indirectly—but from the watchful care which every man has over his own interests, in a given state of things.

Political economy, in all its accidental bearings and in its scope, is, indeed, deep water for any man to dive into; but there are certain practical principles, applicable to this question, which may be obvious to all minds. First, slave property is the capital of the slave States. No dispute about that, as a general truth, and sufficiently comprehensive to decide the question now before us. Consequently, it is this property which gives value to all other property. Take it away, without a fair consideration, without indemnification, and all that portion of the United States is ruined. This is the nutshell of the matter, and comprehends it all.

"No, no," it is said: "the same bone, and muscle, and sinews are there." Nay, but you have changed the whole machinery of society; you have revolutionized it; you have put the master in the power of the quondam slave, and constituted the latter master over the former, without leaving the quondam master a penny in his pocket, unless peradventure, by some good luck, here and there one may have an interest somewhere else beyond the reach of your rapacity. Even with a fair and full indemnification in the present master's hand, or subject to his order, after such a revolution; and in the midst of its disorders and unsettled condition of things, it would be, as we think, somewhat more than enough to baffle ordinary wisdom and perseverance to establish permanently and comfortably that new and untried state of society, that would be required; and it is not unlikely, that enough would abandon the attempt in discouragement,—seeking a better fortune in other States and Territories of the Union—to leave the residue inadequate to sustain the interests of the several Commonwealths thus deserted, in any degree of prosperity. They might dwindle and decline, till all would be glad to be out of them, if they could conscientiously. This is purely a question of domestic and political economy, that would depend on the practical workings of such a system. If this were the only field open before them, then they would all be compelled to stay, and put to their strength, and make the best of it. But we know, that men are always governed by their interests, and habits, as to where they will stay or go.

Certainly, we do not present the doubtfulness of such a prospect, pending on such contingencies, as an objection to the measure; but as one that claims to be considered in this discussion, that will of course be considered by the parties immediately concerned. It is impossible to determine beforehand how many influences, in such a new state of things, might operate to their discouragement or the contrary, or what would be the balance of those influences on either side, after each shall have been neutralized by each, to the extent of their action. It is sufficiently obvious, however, that they would require all the capital invested in a fair indemnification for the property resigned, to work such a system advantageously. It would be enough, and probably more than many of them could well endure, to change all their habits of society and of living so entirely as the new system would require; and those who could not satisfactorily accommodate themselves to it, would of course emigrate—and a general disposition to emigrate would probably involve political ruin—that is, ruin absolute; for nothing is better for mankind, in their associated capacity, than political prosperity, and nothing worse than political adversity.

Admitting, then, that the effects of the operation of such a system on the internal condition, absolute wealth, and political prosperity of the present slave States, would present the result as *simply doubtful,* as to what it would be with the capital of indemnification available on the premises—what would it be without any indemnification at all? We think this question might fairly be set down as the end of the story and of the argument. Every practical man must see, that it would be beggary and ruin; and that the entire field must be abandoned to the colored race, now there, to set up such a state of society as they might be able, unless the Government of the United States, in charity, should take it in charge as an immense poor house, to make the best of it they could—the white population in the mean time, reduced to poverty, and going out where they might, to begin the world anew.

But do the Abolitionists say, "These are questions we never regard ourselves as bound to consider, and consequences with which we have nothing to do." But gentlemen, you *are* bound to consider these questions; you *cannot* rid yourselves of the responsibility of these consequences, if the work that produces them be yours. "But, *no matter* what becomes of the master, so the slave be free; if the master *should* be ruined, he has well deserved it." *Say* this, gentlemen, but *once*—say it *openly, fairly, publicly,* that the world may understand you—and we think, that will be enough.

But do the Abolitionists still say, "We can neither talk nor treat with persons or parties, who speak of '*slave property,*' of property in the persons of men, a thing not possible *to be,* and an idea not to be tolerated for a moment, wherever, and whatever authority, may have usurped it." This may be a very good reason why they should not talk *at all* on the subject, since it is a simple matter of fact, which constitutes the matter and ground of controversy. We hope we have a proper respect for scruples of conscience, and that we are sufficiently unwilling to disturb nervous sensitiveness; but we have not forgotten honest Joe's definition of his own conscience, in a certain case, when hardly pressed, viz. "I wont." Nothing would more effectually put a party in argument, *hors de combat,* than such logic. There is really no getting at them; and yet they insist on having to do with the matter. We have probably as great an aversion to *the thing* signified by these terms, as the Abolitionists; at least, we used to have, and we have seen no good reason for a change of sentiment. But for the practical purposes of so great a theme, if we think fit to meddle with it, we see not how such language can be avoided, as it is indispensable to set forth the facts of the case.

But, if the Abolitionists prefer to foreclose debate, by saying, "We lay our hands upon our swords, in the presence of all persons, who shall presume thus to insult humanity, and assume this defiance in the presence of the country, and before the world, as to the cause in which we are engaged, the Constitution and the laws of the land and the Government and all the slave States to the contrary notwithstanding," there is of course an end of logic, and of "free discussion;" and their position would be well understood, under such a frank avowal. But we cannot say, that we are prepared to commend it; although we are unable to see, how this violent setting aside of the only terms of debate, through the medium of which the subject can be approached, and yet urging forward the irresistible momentum of their tremendous machinery on the parties most intimately concerned in this question, is much short of this.

CHAPTER XVIII
THE CONDITION OF AMERICAN SLAVES AS COMPARED WITH OTHER PORTIONS OF THE AFRICAN RACE

There is nothing but the most *enlarged* view of a great question, that can fairly determine its merits; and it cannot be denied, that slavery is *one* of the great questions appertaining to the social state of mankind, and to the political state of the world. It is so great, in our opinion, that it can neither be disposed of by the logic of visionary theorists, nor by a *coup du main* of an ill-considered and intemperate effort, nor by any legerdemain of political quackery. Ever since human society was set up, so far as history deposes, slavery has been a component element in one form or another. We suppose, there are some good reasons for saying, that there is no institution—we beg pardon of the Abolitionists for using this term, and assure them that we mean nothing by it but the fact—none, that can assert a more ancient date, except that of matrimony, and the natural relations accruing therefrom; and none that has been more uninterrupted, since it was first set up. Reason might teach us, therefore, that a custom thus sanctioned by time and the history of human society, so deeply rooted, so thoroughly interwoven, and incorporated with the social fabric of large portions of the human family, however wrong it may be, so long as there is not a uniform opinion on the subject among those who have the charge of it, cannot be eradicated and put out of the way by a single blow.

We are aware, that the Abolitionists have published some very strong and significant doctrines, intended to be applied to the evils of the social system. For example in their last Annual Report:—"The very *vitality* of human society for these six thousand years, has consisted in the victories of certain institutions over others—*of the new over the old*—of the better over the worse—just as the heart, by successive tides of regenerated blood, chases corruption and death from the bodily system. Tyranny in all ages, has striven to carry this moral (political) non-intercourse (non-interference) law into practice, but never with success. Had it succeeded, where would have been our Christianity and its successive reformations?" &c. Who would not say, "Good Lord deliver us" from the operation of a principle, thus boldly avowed, which asserts the right and necessity of everlasting revolution! and which plants itself on the platform, *that might is right*! Christianity itself is not protected from its invading sweep: "its successive *reformations*!" Where is the man in history, or living, that can lay claim to have *reformed*, or now to *reform*, Christianity? The very suggestion is blasphemous. And yet, it would seem, an act of this kind is even now, and among us, proposed to be enacted, because, forsooth, Christianity, after all "its reformations" and improvements, is not quite bold enough, is rather doubtful, and has even thrown out some suggestions a little adverse to the necessities of present exigencies!

But to return: Abolition simply, and in itself considered, is not the only question to be discussed, as the whole matter now presents itself to the mind of the public, and claims consideration. The phasis of the subject comprehends the broad disk of society. The Abolitionists have forced their opponents to this wide view, by having set the example. They have brought up so many questions, and implicated so many principles, as to have set aside the main question; at least have thrown it into the back ground, so that the term Abolition no longer suggests alone the primitive idea of emancipation, nor hardly suggests it at all; but arrays before the mind a *system* of principles, social and political, which are regarded by most people as of a very revolting character. It is impossible to meet such a foe without taking into consideration the ground which he occupies, without reconnoitring and surveying his position. He has already betrayed the poor slave, vitiated his cause, rivetted his chains, made all his prospects more hopeless, put far off the day of his emancipation, and at last run foul of a precipitous, frowning, and immoveable rock, that is likely to sit long in dignified composure on the base of the eternal hills, while the assailant exhausts his energies and breaks his sides by dashing against the rude and projecting points below.

The opponents of Abolition principles, therefore, are treated very unfairly when they are of course set down as opposed to emancipation. This latter question cannot now be taken up, till the battle is concluded in defence of other and more momentous principles, for the subversion of which a disciplined army of Destructives has rushed into the field. Nevertheless, so long as the Abolitionists continue to hold up the slave—whose prospects they have ruined, till he gets better help—as a shield for the accomplishment of other ends, it still remains necessary to give reasons why emancipation cannot be brought about with that precipitate haste which the Abolitionists propose.

We design, however, in this chapter, not to aim directly at the point above suggested, but to present somewhat of the *comparative condition* of the slaves in the United States, principally in relation to the history of the African race, since, at the time, and previous to the time, when the slave trade commenced, with the purpose of coming fairly to the conclusion, whether their condition in this country is an improvement or deterioration; and consequently, whether, in the Providence of God, and in their social right, as a distinct and separate race, they have a fair claim to the instant elevation among the people of this country, which the Abolitionists demand for them, if it can be obtained only at the expense of social order, and at the peril of our institutions.

First, we observe, that the African race, in the Middle, Western, and more Southern parts of the Continent, have for many centuries, or from time immemorial, been most barbarous and degraded, and in the practice of domestic slavery on the largest scale and in the most inhuman forms, entirely independent of the effects of the slave traffic by exportation from Africa to America.

"It is evident," says Mungo Park, "that the system of slavery which prevails in Africa is of *no modern date*. It probably had its origin in the remote ages of antiquity, before the Mohammedans explored a path across the desert. How far it is maintained and supported by the slave traffic, which for two hundred years the nations of Europe have carried on with the natives of the Coast, it is neither within my province, nor in my power to explain. If my sentiments should be desired concerning the effect of a discontinuance of this commerce on the manners of the natives, *I should have no hesitation in saying*, that in the present unenlightened state of their minds, *my opinion is, the effect would neither be so extensive nor so beneficial as many wise and worthy persons fondly expect.*"

Park estimates the domestic slavery of Africa, on an average, at *three fourths*, and Lander at *four fifths*, of the population. Some travellers have gone much higher, and we have seen it put down at *nine tenths*.

"In a speech delivered in the British House of Commons, by Mr. Henniker, in 1789, the speaker asserts, that a letter had been received by George III. from one of the most powerful of the African potentates, the Emperor of Dehomey, which exemplifies the notions of the Africans about the right to kill and enslave prisoners of war. He (the Emperor) stated: 'That as he understood King George was the greatest of white kings, so he thought himself the greatest of black ones.' He said, that he could lead 500,000 armed men into the field, that being the pursuit to which *all* his subjects were bred, the women *only* staying at home to plant and manure the earth. He had himself fought *two hundred and nine battles*, with great reputation and success, and had conquered the great king of Ardah. The king's head was to this day preserved with the flesh and hair; the heads of his generals were distinguished by being placed on each side of the doors of their Fetiches; with the heads of the inferior officers they paved the space before the doors; and the heads of the common soldiers formed a sort of fringe or outwork round the walls of the palace. Since this war he had experienced the greatest good fortune; and he hoped in good time to be able to complete the outwalls of all his great houses, *to the number of seven, in the same manner.*

"Mr. Norris, who visited this Empire, testifies to the truth of this letter. He found the palace of the Emperor an immense assemblage of cane and mud tents, enclosed by a high wall. The skulls and jaw bones of enemies slain in battle, formed the favorite ornaments of the palaces and *temples.* The king's apartments were paved, and the walls and roofs stuck over, with these horrid trophies. *And if a farther supply appeared at any time desirable, he announced to his general*, that his house wanted thatch, *when a war for that purpose was immediately undertaken.*"[10]

[10] Professor Dew's Review &c.

"All these unfortunate beings," prisoners of war, says Park, "are considered as strangers and foreigners, *who have no right to the protection of the law*, and may be treated with severity, or sold to a stranger, according to the pleasure of their owners. There are indeed, regular markets, where slaves of this description are bought and sold; and the value of a slave in the eye of an African purchaser increases in proportion to the distance from his native kingdom; for, when slaves are only a few days journey from the place of their nativity, they frequently effect their escape; but when one or more kingdoms intervene, escape being more difficult, they are more readily reconciled to their situation. On this account the unhappy slave is often transferred from one dealer to another, until he has lost all hope of returning to his native kingdom.

"A battle is fought; the vanquished never think of rallying again; the inhabitants become panic-struck; and the conquerors have only to bind the slaves, and carry off the victims and their plunder. Such of their prisoners as through age or infirmity are unable to endure fatigue, or are found unfit for sale, are considered useless, *and I have no doubt are put to death. The same fate commonly awaits chiefs, or any other persons who have taken a distinguished part in the war.*"

The Rev. Stephen Kay, Corresponding member of the South African Institution &c., gives a most heart rending account of the horrid barbarities of war; of the great extent and atrocities of slavery; of the extreme degradation and hardships of females, who are always regarded and treated as slaves, and no longer valued when they become useless; of modes of torture and killing too shocking to be narrated; all of which, and many other atrocities of African barbarism, are the common scenes of those regions of Africa which he visited. Major Laing is to the same point, and various other travellers that have found motives to visit Africa, or to penetrate into its interior. There is no diversity of testimony on the subject, but one common voice going out upon the world, through a variety of channels, running back for ages, and from numerous and remote sections of that dark and cruel Continent, all certifying to their extreme barbarism and brutal degredation, with scarcely a gleam of intellectual light, or social comfort, beaming out from their history. Do not the readers of Mungo Park recollect the story of poor Nealee? Does not the world know the fate of Park himself, and of Lander? And are not the testimonies abundant to the barbarous treachery and atrocious cruelty of the race, independent of the effects of that European traffic in human flesh and blood, which began, between two and three hundred years ago, to draw off a fraction of this immense amount of human misery, which could scarcely be increased by the agonies and suffocations of "the middle passage"? It was, indeed, this very state of things which presented temptations and opened the door to that traffic, which transplanted a portion of the African race to the Islands and Continent of this Western hemisphere. It is to the Africans themselves, that this trade owes its origin—to their barbarism, to their everlasting trade in war, and the glutting of their own marts with the blood and sinews of their own flesh all to the sore evil of this Continent, and to the inexpiable scandal of Christian Europe, that the flood gates of African barbarism were let out upon these Western Isles and shores, to gratify the lust of gain in those monsters who carried on and profited by the traffic, and to entail a long protracted curse on the less guilty, though not innocent, tenants of this new world.

The continuance of this traffic, and the inhuman over-working of this race in the South American and West Indian Colonies appertaining to the Governments of Europe, are too notorious to require recitation. We are more concerned to notice the history and character of that slavery which is to be found in our own Republic, as the result of that trade which disgraced Christendom, and imposed on the Nations that tolerated and patronized it a fearful responsibility.

Now, what we have to say, in reference to the facts and general allusions appertaining to the history of the African race, comprehensively stated in this chapter, the truth and fairness of which we presume will not be drawn in question, is for the simple purpose of comparison. It is not to apologize for slavery; it is not to palliate, in any degree, the guilt of those agents who introduced it to this Continent; it is not to justify the principle of slavery; it is not to extenuate any of its evils; but simply to determine the question, so far as it may be obvious in the lights of such comparison, whether that portion of the African race to be found in the United States, are actually better off than they would have been any where else, in all reasonable probability?

We think, then, we are prepared to say, that when all the evils of slavery in the Southern States of this country are put together, without abatement in the smallest item; when the domestic slave trade is posted and summed up in all its worst features and worst consequences; when all the overworking of the prœdul slave is brought into the account, with its attendant cruelties; when the driving system, so far as it exists, and all arbitrary severities of discipline for offences, are considered; and nothing of evil that belongs to the whole system in the United States be left out, the fair conclusion will be, that the whole sum is but a small fraction of the same classes of evils that from time immemorial have belonged and still belong to the barbarism of the father land of this race—not reckoning other evils, scarcely to be told for their number, or estimated for their enormity or magnitude, to be found there, but not to be found here.

Although the difference is not of the same kind, nor probably so great, still the comparison of the slavery of the United States with that which has existed in the West Indies and other parts of America, presents the former in the light of comparative comfort and happiness. It may be said, indeed, that in the British West Indies, the quondam slaves, so cruelly treated and so severely overworked, have at last come to their freedom; but it is by far too soon to estimate the result. In St. Domingo, where they have been free, or said to be free, nearly a half century, they are still under "overseers," and "drivers," still subject to the law of "passports," still forced to work a specific number of hours on penalty of fines, imprisonments, and sundry severe modes of discipline, under "the *Code rural*" and "the *Code Henri*," differing in despotic character only, that the people are slaves to the Government, and not to private owners, and driven to work by a black man instead of a white man, when universally they prefer the white, as being more merciful of the two. The three great staples of Hayti fell off from 1791 under the French, to 1822 under Boyer: Sugar from 163,405,220 lbs. annually to 652,541 lbs.; Coffee from 68,151,180 lbs. annually to 35,117,834 lbs.; and Cotton from 6,286,126 lbs. annually to 891,950 lbs.; and have since declined, till the public revenue has fallen below the expenditures of the Government.

We see, then, that the *evils* of American slavery are *blessings* as compared with the general fate of the African race in their native Continent, independent of the effects of the exportation of slaves to foreign parts; and that they are light in comparison of other foreign servitude down to this date.

Let us now turn to the scale of comparative comfort and of actual privilege. In the first place, American slaves are placed in the midst of a high state of civilization, where their very bondage has rights secured by law which would be a blessing in Africa, even after deducting the entire scope of the arbitrary sway of masters. They are clustered round a refinement of manners, which, though it may have little influence for the benefit of the prœdal slave, acts powerfully on the great body for their personal improvement and elevation in the scale of intellectual and moral being, and remotely has a favorable effect upon all. A great portion of them have been admitted to no inconsiderable degrees of intellectual and moral culture; domestic and body servants are often found highly improved and accomplished, whose principles, morals, and manners would be a good example to a large part of our white population; the privileges of the Gospel, and its blessed and eternal hopes, have been brought within the reach of a greater proportion of the slaves, than of the white population, who customarily *use* them, when brought to their doors, and these privileges were being still farther extended till the crusade of the Abolitionists caused them to be abridged; the system of American slavery makes it the interest of the master to be careful of the physical constitution of the slave, that it should not be impaired, and in this particular makes it preferable to the more cruel bondage of British manufactories; American masters are compelled by law to maintain the sick, the infirm, and the aged; the law itself enacts penalties for inhuman treatment, and public opinion sustains it, notwithstanding that in this, as in all states of society, the law may be better than the practice, still, however, it has its general influence for the protection of the slave, and demands justice for him when abused as well as for the abused white man; many of the slaves of this country have emerged, and are constantly emerging, from a state of bondage to a state of freedom, till they amount to about one sixth of the colored population, and are admitted to important civil, social, and religious privileges, though not to all which the Abolitionists claim for them, yet important and invaluable as compared with what they would have been likely to enjoy any where else; the public opinion of this country, previous to the present Abolition agitation, not excepting even that of the slave States, had been constantly growing more favourable to an increased amelioration of slavery, and to ultimate emancipation.

In a word: If we take into consideration the origin of this race, the barbarism, the brutal degradation, and the customary inhuman vices of their ancestry, which remain the same to this day in Africa; if we look at the different conditions and fate of other portions of the same race, who, in consequence of such a state of things in the land of their fathers, have been carried away from their native shores; and then compare the whole with the general progress of nations and tribes in human improvement over the face of the earth, we shall, as we think, be compelled to the conclusion, that no other people can be found on the globe, civilized or uncivilized, who have, within the same period of time, risen so much, or been improved so much, as a body, in their actual condition, social character, privileges, relations, and prospects, for time and for eternity, as that portion of the African race now to be found in the United States of North America.

Let it not be understood or said, that we adduce this *great fact*, as a bar to any claims that may be fairly asserted by the colored people of this country, bond or free, or in their behalf, to still farther improvement; but only, that it is proper—that in present circumstances, we are bound—to take the most enlarged view of so great a question; that we are bound to consider, as human nature is, and in such a world as ours, that all nations and tribes, in their best estate, necessarily advance in improvement by *degrees*; that one tribe or nation cannot claim to rise at the expense of another, more especially when their own vices have put them at the bottom of the scale; and that all must fall in with the fair, proper, and unavoidable influence of time, events, and accidental circumstances, over which society, in a regular and constituted course of action, has no control. To insist on breaking in upon this general and conventional movement by violence, on disturbing the established order of human society, to force forward one race, one nation, one tribe, and one class, at the expense of another, and in violation of the recognized principles and actual frame of society, is treason to society, and to the general rights of mankind. The time of absolute *perfectionism*, either as to individual character, or as to the structure of human society, in our opinion, has not yet come. And while all are anxious for improvement, public and private, and are striving for it, all must consent to carry it forward on recognized principles—on principles which will not tear down society, and subvert and overthrow important advantages and vital interests already acquired for common good.

We say, then, as much as we sympathize with the colored population of this country—and we solemnly aver, that we are not wanting in such sympathy—in all that they are deprived of social advantages and political privileges enjoyed by the white population, in all that they fall below the most satisfactory standard and elevation in human improvement—we say, that we do not see how they can fairly claim to rise by *one step* to such a desirable point, contrary to the usual modes of progress in human society, and contrary to the known laws and capabilities of human nature, if it must be to the disturbance of the peace of the community, and to the great peril of our Government and its institutions. We have seen, that the colored population of this country, as a body, have not been injured, but benefitted, by the position which they now occupy, not only in comparison with the history of the race to which they belong, but also in comparison with the common history of other tribes and nations. They undoubtedly occupy at this moment the highest point of actual comfort, of social condition, and of general privilege, which has yet fallen to the lot of any portion of the African race.

We have now done with this branch of the subject, and have only to add, that we shall be treated with great injustice, if these considerations are received as having been offered for any other purpose than a shield alike to the social and political fabric of our country against violence, and to the best interests of the colored race.

CHAPTER XIX
THE EXAMPLE OF QUAKERS,
OR SOCIETY OF FRIENDS

The Quakers have generally received credit for being a peace-loving and peace-making Society of Christians; and we are compelled to admit, and have great pleasure in doing so, that they have always sustained the character. They have always been known as the opponents of slavery; but their modes of protest and remonstrance have been conducted in the spirit of Christianity. They have never broken the public peace, directly or indirectly, in this conflict of principle; they have never outraged public feeling by obtruding their opinions in a violent way; they have not sought to raise mobs against themselves, and thus get the advantage of a cry of persecution; but they have published their principles in a quiet, and in that way, most influential manner. All the world has known, that the Society of Friends have been opposed to slavery, as well as to war; but society has never been battered by their artillery, by violent and uncharitable denunciation, by defamation, by exaggerated and fictitious stories, by inflammatory appeals, by threatening to overthrow a fabric which they cannot conscientiously support, by undermining the authority of Government and proclaiming it forfeited, and by sowing the seeds of servile insurrection and popular violence. It is known, that a Quaker will not eat sugar or molasses made by a slave; that is a fact that tells—sets people to thinking. It is the silent, insinuating action of principle on society and into the minds of men. The Quakers will do nothing, directly or indirectly, to countenance and support slavery, so far as they can avoid it. Their precepts are known, and their example is seen. They are a living epistle before the world, on this and some other subjects. They use freedom of speech and of the press; they employ persuasion and remonstrance in a Christian like way; they give "line upon line, precept upon precept, here a little, and there a little;" but they do no violence. They are faithful and true to their principles, and consistent in practising as well as preaching them; but they assume not the responsibility of disturbing others in the use of a privilege which is so important and dear to themselves. They seem to understand the rule: "Do unto others, as ye would that others should do unto you." Hence the Quakers never disturb the peace of society. They are good neighbours, good citizens, good, we presume, in domestic and private life, and as we hope, good Christians.

Such is the legitimate action of Christianity, and such is the strongest possible proof, that a man is actuated by Christian principle. Such was the example of Christ and his Apostles. There is not a single intimation, nor fair inference from any fact, that they ever made war upon the existing fabric of society, any farther than the silent action of their principles would *gradually* operate a change in the social state and in social institutions. Such is the Divine superiority of Christianity: silent, but effective and irresistable in its march—irresistable, *because* it is never violent—because, veritas valebit, truth will prevail.

But, alas! how utterly opposed to all this are the measures and movements of the Abolitionists! They seem as if they would take heaven and earth by storm; but if they happen to raise a storm over their own heads, they demand impunity from its effects. Stirrers-up of mischief, they deny the right of its re-action on themselves. It is ridiculous, absolutely. If a man will be a fool, he must *reap* his folly; if "he sows the wind," he must be content, if the elements in their natural workings should so decree, "to reap the whirlwind."

If, indeed, we have given more credit to the Quakers than they deserve, we hope, if any of them have got out of the way into the Abolition ranks under their present flag, they will see the propriety of getting back again as fast as they can, for the good reputation of their own Society, that hereafter there may be no exception among them as a good example worthy of imitation in all such matters.

CHAPTER XX
THE SOUTH HAVE DONE WITH ARGUMENT

"Yea, doubtless," saith the Abolitionist, "for reason fails them." And so we have all done with argument; for we shall not stop to reply to this. "The South know their rights," said a Southern gentleman the other day on the floor of Congress, very significantly, and in relation to this subject. This, we believe, is the present common feeling of the slaveholding States. They have made up their minds; and we think they will have the sympathy of the reasonable part of mankind. Their present attitude is that of pointing the people of this country to the bulwark of the Federal Constitution; and if that will not protect them, "they know their rights." We do not quote this language to expose the Southerners to the charge of holding up a menace; for we do not accept it as such, and think it would be unfair for any body to do so. They stand on the defensive; they have been assailed, and are yet assailed; they have felt themselves insulted on the floor of Congress by indirect attempts to invade their rights of State sovereignty; they have been compelled to special legislation and other public action to defend their own territories from violation; they have dreamed of seeing their wives and children butchered, and their houses pillaged and burned; they have seen, in imagination, and as a natural consequence of the Abolition movement unresisted and unchecked, all these and many other horrors of a like kind, enacted before their eyes; they have seen the Government upturned, society dissolved, and anarchy stalking amid the triumphs of its own desolation over their fields; and with such prospects before them, as the result of a foreign interference, organized in open violation of the laws of the land, and in the face of a solemn national compact forbidding such aggression, and engaging to protect and defend them against it, are they not entitled to say—"We know our rights?" How long must they suffer—how long must they be menaced by such invasion, before they may say, we will suffer it no longer? A day of anxiety is as a year of torment; a year of such suspense, is as an age of agony.

And what will they do? Why, clearly, break loose from the Union, to which, generally, they have already made up their minds, in case of necessity, they being judges—if the straws in the wind are any sure indication of its career—"Necessity needs no law." If the Government of the country will not protect them, they must protect themselves, or try to do so. They may fail, and prove impotent; but when men are insulted and outraged, especially the men of the South, they are not nice calculators of consequences; and it is for us of the North to determine, whether we are willing to see our brethren of the South driven to such a resort, by the continued action of an unlawful combination, that exists and has grown up among ourselves; whether, indeed, we are willing to see the Government of this proud Republic rent asunder by such a cause, and to hazard the consequences.

If any body thinks these remarks are not well founded, we are sorry they are not better observers of the symptomatic phenomena of our own society. If they should think them unreasonable and out of place, we are sorry for that also, as we have judged otherwise, and take leave to invite their attention to the next chapter.

CHAPTER XXI
REASONS WHY THE ABOLITION MOVEMENT, UNDER ITS PRESENT ORGANIZATION, MUST SUCCEED IN OVERTHROWING THE GOVERNMENT

We do not believe, after what has taken place, that the Abolitionists will be able to carry *emancipation*. Their imprudent and rash modes of action seem to have barred the door effectually against that event for the present. We think it reasonable to say, that without the concurrence of the slave States, such an event is impossible. But such is the character, effectiveness, and irresistible sweep of their organization, that it cannot fail to break down something; and that something, we fear, will be the Federal Union. We now propose to give our reasons for this apprehension. Those reasons are embodied in the unconstitutional and illegal character of the Association.

The political structure of our Government cannot be too much admired for the balance of power which is every where to be found in its Constitutional modes of action. The theory seems to be a perfect one. But the moment there is a departure from the rules, or a violation of the principles of Constitutional law, the machinery is embarrassed, and danger threatens. In the same manner as the action of the Government demands a strict adherence to these rules, so also does the action of the people. We have seen in the second chapter what rules the Federal Constitution and those of the States prescribe to individual and popular action for political purposes, independent of and in addition to the privilege of the elective franchise: freedom of speech and of the press, and the right of petition, address, and remonstrance to the Government. It was there stated, that the license given to these proscribed forms constituted equally a law of prohibition to all *other* forms, as it would be absurd to suppose, that a written law of this kind is not a law of limitation; in other words, that it is no law at all. It was also shown, as is manifest at first sight, that this license is all sufficient, as the people always have their remedy in the elective franchise, if the Government do not regard their wishes, as expressed in these modes. No occasions can be expected to occur, that would require to transcend these salutary rules; and we believe the existence and action of the American Anti-Slavery Society, as an independent political body, is the first instance, in the history of our country, by which they have been transcended.

It is true, indeed, that a popular charge has been brought against the Masonic Institution, as having been perverted into political action, and as being dangerous to the liberties of the country on that account. How far this charge is just, it is impossible for us to know, as we have never been a member of that Society. It is sufficient to observe, that the very suspicion of such action has operated, as is well known, almost entirely to suppress that Institution, and wind up its history in the country. Had the truth of this charge been obvious, and as susceptible of proof, as in the case of the American Anti-Slavery Society, we need not say what would have been its fate. The legislation of the country would have settled the matter soon. We believe it to be a self-evident proposition, that the genius of a Constitutional Government, or of any government whatever, does not admit of a rival independent political organization on the same territory; that it cannot tolerate *any permanent* political organization *at all* independent of itself; much less one of unlimited powers. It would not be very acceptable, even if it were to come in as an auxiliary, but would rather be regarded as an insult. There is no point of view in which we can conceive it would be welcome.

It would be ridiculous and impotent to say, that the action of the American Anti-Slavery Society cannot be liable to objection, since it is open, and not secret, like the Masonic Institution, admitting that the latter is fairly accused by popular suspicion. Such a plea would justify the acts of fraud, theft, felony, and crime of any description, if they be done openly. It is only the more astonishing, that it should be endured. But the reason of that we have already stated: It is a new thing under the Sun; the public have been taken by surprise; and have not even yet recovered from the shock. It was taken for granted, that religion could not find its way into the State over such Constitutional barriers erected to intercept the trespass; and yet it is there—the religion of a *Sect*—of a great, powerful, fanatical, religioso-political sect—which, having leaped the wall, has carried with it a great and powerful political machinery from another region, and is well at work, as if it were perfectly at home. It may be said, that the political world has never yet had such a fellow worker before, and looks at it askance as a strange companion, not knowing what to make of it. Doubtless, after a little reflection, a more definite opinion will be formed of its unwelcome character and awkward position.

But, it is proper to exhibit more distinctly the beautiful and symmetrical action of the Constitutional law of this land, when scrupulously observed in regard to such matters, and how a departure from it leads to difficulty. It will be seen, that freedom of speech and of the press, and the right of petition, address, and remonstrance to Government, as guaranteed, are important safety valves, through which to give scope to individual opinion, and vent to popular fermentations. The regular action of these powers in the Constitutional modes, and through the Constitutional channels, are always balanced by each other. That same freedom of speech and of the press which is guaranteed to one individual or party, is guaranteed to another; and the inordinate excesses of each are sure to be counteracted by the ordinary sway of these Constitutional principles; at least, so far as the imperfect state of society will allow. It seems to be the highest attainment of a practical political sagacity. In the same manner, the action of associated popular movements, when they aim to affect and influence the Government, is always balanced by the counteraction of one party as opposed to the other, so long as both keep within the prescribed forms of the Constitution and laws, and connect themselves regularly with the Government in the recognized modes of petition, address, or remonstrance. In this way it is impossible that one party should gain a sudden, undue, and overwhelming advantage, to which they are not fairly entitled by the merits of their cause, and by a fair hearing before the public.

But the moment that one party, or any new party, is permitted to set up an independent, permanent, and unconstitutional political machinery, having no connexion with the Government, but acting under a polity of its own, as much and as truly as an independent empire, and thus instituting a mode of action unknown to the Constitution and laws, this salutary equipoise of influence is lost, in the same manner as by throwing an ounce weight into one of two scales equally balanced, the other is made to kick the beam. Such is the character, and such the overbearing power of the American Anti-slavery Society in the political condition of our country. There is, there can be, no balance of influence, apart from the interference of authority, except by setting up another unconstitutional organization, to put aside the Constitutional Government, to carry on the war between themselves, and settle the questions in dispute, as best they might; in other words, to establish the reign of anarchy.

So long as the American Anti-slavery Society is permitted to exist, and to carry on its operations under its present form, it is not the reason of their cause that prevails, but the power of their machinery in its action on the public mind. All opposing influences, so long as the Government is inactive, are like the scattering, random, and over-shoulder shot of a routed and retreating host that is flying in the field before the well-formed, steady, and disciplined march of a triumphant army—triumphant, because there is no corresponding agency to oppose them, not because they have the right. Such, precisely, is the effect of all the newspaper squibs that are fired off on the Abolitionists, and such the effect of the unorganized remonstrances of the public. The Abolitionists are in the field with a disciplined army, officered, paid, with a full staff, and an adequate Commissariat. In other words, they are a regularly organized and permanent political body, acting under a complete State machinery in all that their exigences require, adding to it at pleasure, with ever active and industrious agents, with money at command and the power of the press, and as independent of the Government of this country as the throne of the Sultan at Constantinople—and yet doing the business of the country!

There are most obvious reasons, why such a power, once recognized as suitable and proper, will carry all before it, till it shall have dissolved the Government of this country. The Abolitionists have all the native and long cherished feeling of the North on their side, as being opposed to slavery in principle; they have all the advantage of the sympathies of our nature, when we consider the *manner* in which they represent the case; they have the common and prevailing popular ignorance of the nature of our political fabric to aid them—for it is not to be supposed, that the people generally will have clear and uniform views on a question upon which Statesmen differ; and to the effect of all these natural and social auxiliaries, they superadd the power of their immense, combined, and variously ramified machinery, which steals every where upon the public, catching every man, woman, and child, whose benevolent sympathies are naturally open to their appeals, and when once they are indoctrinated after the manner and in the school of the Abolitionists, and become possessed of their spirit, there is little chance for the sway of those principles on which our political society is based. It is not the fair argument of the cause, but the power of this political combination, that bears such sway. There is no chance for a candid hearing before the public, and for the due influence of all the considerations which appertain to this momentous and complicated question, because the constitutional balance of power, designed for such exigences, has been prostrated by an usurpation, and every thing is made to give way to isolated and abstract opinions, and to the dictations of political quackery. Fanaticism rules, and not reason; and the natural and inevitable consequence will be, that the gradual accumulation of this moral power, thus acquired, will swell to a magnitude, and urge on a momentum, before the pressure of which the Union will be compelled to yield and break down. The people of the South will be annoyed and vexed, till they can be annoyed and vexed no longer. Then will be the beginning of the end.

Are we understood? Is it not clear, that it is this political usurpation of an unlawful power, that puts the country in peril? Let this irregularity, this transcending of law, be reduced again to the Constitutional basis, and all this excitement, alarm, and danger, will die away, because the healthful Constitutional balance of influence would be restored. Opinion would then encounter opinion on common ground, with no undue advantage of one party over another.

"But, then," say the Abolitionists, "we must give up our cause." It will have an equal chance with any other. "But," they add, "we have nine points of the law against the Constitution: actual possession of the field, and do not choose to give it up." We are quite aware, that usurpation will always hold on to its unlawfully acquired power, as long as it can; and it is not to be expected, that the Abolitionists will readily concede, that they have been guilty of such a fault. It is a novel experiment in the history of our country; and as to its form, novel in the history of political society. Religion has often usurped political power, and the Constitutional frame of our Government has taken great pains to guard against it; but, we will venture to say, that no human foresight ever anticipated a trespass of this kind: that, by an independent organization of its own devising, religion should come armed into the field, to eject the previous occupants by force—not to divide power and the spoils, but to take sole possession, and set up a new order of things to its own will.

We shall be as stout an advocate for the political rights of religionists of all persuasions, as any body; at the same time we are not prepared to concede to them the right of an independent political organization, in violation of the law, to disturb the peace, endanger the Government, and overthrow the institutions of the country. That the Abolitionists have been guilty of this trespass, we are sorry, because the country is the sufferer; that they should be compelled to tread back, and resign their ill gotten power, we shall be glad, because we believe, that law, propriety, and the good of the country, require it. We believe, too, that the good of the slaves, and the welfare of the free colored people, require it.

CHAPTER XXII
THE ABOLITION ORGANIZATION
DESTRUCTIVE OF REPUBLICAN LIBERTY

If the main argument of this work is sound—and we are unable to see why it is not—the tables are fairly turned on the Abolitionists, who have been crying out for freedom, and the freedom of the Constitution. Enough, we trust, has been said, in the progress of these discussions, to show, that the action of the American Anti-Slavery Society, as a grand and permanent political organization, destroys that balance of individual and popular influence, which the Constitutional law of this land was intended to establish, fortify, and secure; and which is, in truth, the grand palladium of our liberties. The chapter immediately preceding brings this matter to a point.

The freedom of speech and of the press, and the rights of popular action, as guaranteed by the Constitution, or Constitutions, are not worth a penny, so long as the agency of such an institution as the American Anti-Slavery society is permitted to be brought into the field against them. For it is overwhelming by the force of its polity. No matter what may be the prevailing feeling of the public, at any given time in regard to it; no matter how many single voices may be raised in remonstrance against the Abolition movement; no matter how many newspapers may blaze away at the common enemy; no matter how many resolutions of rebuke may be passed by the Senate of the Nation; no matter what other forms of action, by whom soever or where soever, may be instituted, within the prescribed forms of the Constitution, to encounter this foe; yet, so long as the Government, which is the only agency that can treat with such an unconstitutional usurpation on equal terms, remains inactive, they will avail nothing. They are all crippled and rendered nugatory by the moral power and irresistible momentum of this regular system of means, under a State machinery, that is brought into the field. The Abolitionists know their power, under such an advantage, and laugh their enemies to scorn. By the influence of their organization, by its constant, systematic, and all pervading action, they expect, and not without reason, to carry all before them in the free States.

All the freedom guaranteed by the Constitution to their opponents is worth nothing in the scale against such a power; it is annihilated. There is no equality of privilege between the parties.

The reason why the public generally have not understood the character of this enemy, is because it came by a sudden leap, by a sort of somerset, from the religious world, with the operations of which the public, as a body, have not concerned themselves. It is in fact a foreign organized power, that has stolen a march on the territories of the Republic, obtained a footing, and gained an alarming ascendancy, before the public were apprized of the fact, or had any true knowledge of the character of the invaders; and such is their overpowering influence, by virtue of a political polity, that the privileges secured by the Constitution and laws, as a means of opposing them, are rendered utterly valueless, in any thing short of the interposition of authority.

How can the private action of individuals, how can the press in its customary forms, how can the resolutions of popular assemblies, of legislative bodies, of Congress itself, counteract the movements of such on organization? They are utterly impotent. Their influence expires with their acts; while that of this Society, on account of its systematic and efficient organization is untiring, assiduous, is every where, lives forever, and is forever augmenting its forces. The American Anti-Slavery Society can command all the money it wants, and money will command agencies of every description; money is the animating soul of every political body.

It is of no use, therefore, that the Constitutional law of this land has secured these sacred privileges, so long and so highly valued, while the same law is transcended and trampled under foot by this antagonist power. All the imagined advantages of this boasted freedom are annihilated by the sweeping claims and prerogatives of this usurpation. All our liberties are but a name, if such an organization may come in, expunge them from the Charter, and abolish their sway, by setting up a power which the Constitution itself cannot contend with, without calling to its aid the arm of authority, because the rules of the Constitution are violated.

Having discharged this duty—a sincere and conscientious duty, as we profess—to the country, to the cause of humanity, and above all, to that God whom we desire to worship and serve, we are content to submit the question to the public, and await their decision, whether, a new DYNASTY, under the form of a RELIGIOSO-POLITICAL ORGANIZATION, shall be permitted to take the field; or whether, the OLD AND CONSTITUTIONAL GOVERNMENT shall stand?